ONLY ONE WAY LEFT

ONLY ONE WAY LEFT

George MacLeod
Founder of the Iona Community

WILD GOOSE PUBLICATIONS

IONA COMMUNITY CLASSICS

Copyright © 1956 & 2005 The Iona Community

First published 1956
2nd edition 1958
3rd edition 2005 by
Wild Goose Publications, Fourth Floor, Savoy House,
140 Sauchiehall Street, Glasgow G2 3DH, UK,
the publishing division of the Iona Community.
Scottish Charity No. SCO03794.
Limited Company Reg. No. SCO96243.

ISBN 1 905010 02 8

Printed by Lightning Source UK, Milton Keynes

CONTENTS

Let us not always say
' Spite of this flesh to-day,
I strove, made head, gained ground upon the whole.'
As the bird wings and sings,
Let us cry ' All good things
Are ours, nor soul helps flesh
More than flesh helps soul.'

—Robert Browning.

Must I utterly renounce all the things about me, that I may be absorbed into Him, or is there any way in which I can devote them and myself to Him, and only know Him the better by filling my place among them ?

—F. D. Maurice.

Everything begins in Mysticism and ends in Politics.—Charles Peguy.

May your spirit and soul and body be preserved entire and without blame at the coming of our Lord Jesus Christ.

Faithful is He that calleth you, who will also do it.—Saint Paul.

EXPLAINING THIS BOOK

The main chapters of this book (3-8) formed The Cunningham Lectures, designed for divinity students, in New College, Edinburgh in 1954. Under the title of *The Auburn Lectures*, and by permission of the Cunningham Trustees, they formed the basis of a longer series at Union Theological Seminary, New York, later the same year. Laity who attended the lectures in both countries were in the forefront of the demand that they be incorporated in book form. This raised problems. Among divinity students one can assume a general acceptance of the thesis that the Christian must be concerned with politics, in his role as citizen. The lectures, accepting that assumption, explore the reasons why this general acceptance does not issue in action to the extent that it should. They also sketch out the consequence of such concern in the worship and work of a local congregation. For the laity, however, to judge by many questions, there seemed the need of two prior considerations: the state of parliamentary democracy in our so called " Christian West " and the general justification for churchmen to be involved.

Thus, precedent to the lectures, two chapters have been additionally devised.

The first is a political forecast—concerned with " the one way of going Left." The second is the general Church prospect— " the one way left " for the Church if in fact she is to continue in her claim to be the guardian of the Christian West.

It is without apology that the two opening chapters are couched in topical and contemporaneous terms. There are books galore on political theory and they are very necessary. There are, rightly, treatises without number on the civic obligations of a Christian. But they both too often share an almost artful avoidance of coming down to brass tacks. They weave wonderful carpets for the abstract thinker. But the common man has to get the carpets tacked down, to live at all in comfort. If the present writer doesn't get the carpet quite square to the proportions of our tent on earth, he at least claims Bible authority for the topical approach. The Social Prophets did not deal with political theory nor with the general obligations of obedience. They dealt with men and their immediate manners in the face of immediate situations. They made stabs at what they thought their very immediate God was saying right then to them with all their praise and blame. Sometimes the impulsive stabs of the prophets merely sprained their wrists, as their daggers clanged on meaningless, resisting rocks. At other times the prophets toppled over as their daggers whistled through unresisting air. But just occasionally they pierced the skin of the Holy Tent. This aperture made it possible to hear the voice of the Living God who answers only furiously seeking men. Thus would they recover a design and lay their carpets to that pattern. Within a decade the carpets would have to be rolled up. Tents would now have to be dismantled, to escape the oncoming foe, or miraculously to return to some delectable spot from which they had thought themselves forever banished. "Our God is a God that moves." Only in the contemporaneous does God converse with men. His very name is "Now": "I am that I am" and "I will be that I will be."

"So the writer actually claims to be a prophet?" asks the reader. Why not? The essence of a Bible prophet is not that he forecasts the future. It is that he fears in his bones what is going to happen if we don't recover God's design right now. Is not this the motivation of every sincere Christian's ordinary actions? "Would God that all the Lord's people were prophets."

In addition to expressing indebtedness to the Cunningham and Auburn Trustees, the writer is grateful to two great mystics of the last and present century. Edward Irving inspired the plan of the lectures. Alan W. Watts inspired the last chapter. Such illustrations as are of value therein come from his recent book *Behold the Spirit*.

CHAPTER ONE

ONE WAY LEFT IN POLITICS

I was frustrated. I had been asked to review two books. One was a symposium by theologians, all coming by different ways to one firm conclusion—that Christians must be involved in politics. What concerned me was that they did not seem to be involved themselves! The other book was *New Fabian Essays*, a symposium by active politicians. Laboriously they tackled all the snags and pitfalls attendant on creating a patterned State, such as alone can ensure the survival of any nation in our closely interlaced world: unified but not united. The essays plunged about seeking to preserve personal freedom without eschewing essential pattern. What concerned me here was that none of the essays had agreement about principle.

I was frustrated. The authorities on principle had not a clue to give on practice. The authorities on practice were in a quagmire for lack of a prior principle.

This is, of course, a description of our modern world. Is the solution to get them round a common table? Unfortunately, not just now. Take the H-bomb. The theologian is so frightened of what his clear principles imply that he accepts the practice of the politicians. The politician is so frightened of where his practice has led that, secretly, he is aghast that the Church has no firm principle to offer, such as might begin to save. Get them together round a common table and, to judge by official pronouncements, it would be the theologian who would be comforting the politician, while the politician (under his breath) would be muttering, "Come, come."

Get them round a common table? Unfortunately, not just now. I know it is easy to write like this; and not much good. Indeed it is positively bad if I give the impression that I sit on some rostrum, distributing bad marks alike to each. So let me hasten to add that I too carry in my own being a similar divorce. Too clearly do I see the Christian principle for my personal

I

contacts, damnably do I fail when it comes to practice. That goes for you too.

I have opened thus brusquely to make two points. Unless they are appreciated we will get nowhere. They are the points which the common man skips as he faces our darkening world, and, in skipping, lands in a bog. So landed, he is apt to stay there deciding " politics are no good." Deciding perhaps to dig an allotment, he buys the seed catalogues instead of books on politics. An increasing number of men do this, though many prefer darts or dominoes to digging. The vast majority are oblivious that such escapist decisions are ominously political. For if their number should greatly increase, it is they who would open the door either to a fascism or a communism, however veiled.

Thus two prior considerations for the understanding of our time—fantastically foreshortened—are that

(1) There is no longer any such thing as a " Christian West," and

(2) This has as serious personal as corporate consequences.

NO LONGER A CHRISTIAN WEST

When the civilised world circled the Mediterranean, man made a recognisable stab at a " Christian Society." There was one Church, the final arbiter of the quarrels of men. There was also a hierarchy of living in which each person had his place, and more often than not his significance, in Society. Though rapacities were great and injustices immense, the concept recognisably worked. Princes could, and did, get together to appeal to the Arbiter when chaos seemed imminent. It worked for a person's dignity too. True, too many were burnt at the stake, but at least a Priest stood beside them to declare the significance of each immortal soul.

Now the whole concept of " Christendom " has gone. Our God is a God that moves.

The Reformation was part of God's plot, but it broke the theory of a central authority. The Renaissance gave birth to a

2

wondrous race of emancipated men. It also gave birth to monsters. The once co-operating states gave way to autonomous nations, each with a State Church. The differing realms of knowledge that had paid homage at the court of Theology, the Queen of the Sciences, moved off into their own little corners, saying " Boo ! " to the Queen. Important here for our present purpose : the rule and management of money set up its own court to become an autonomous activity. These were some of the debits. The credits, of course, were also enormous. The sciences found innumerable truths, to the existence of which the splendour of the Queen had blinded them. Money, freed, made credit creditable and opened up the whole new world. What of Man ? All western men are educated now as princes used to be. And western man (democratic) holds in his vote the authority that princes held on their behalf.

But and but and but—" What is education for ? " That is the question that none can answer with authority. All our western youth are the plaything of a plethora of replies. " What is life about ? " That is anybody's guess. Religion has become the hobby of the few. If a man likes music he goes to the conservatoire. If painting, he seeks out an artist's studio. Or if certain psychic elements predominate in his make-up he " takes up " God. The real trouble is that the Bible is not about that sort of religion at all. In the Bible, God is a total Sovereign not a personal solace. Authentic solace resides in a serious acceptance of His total sovereignty. God is at the hub round which the whole wheel of life revolves. If we make of Him a spiritual hobby, we end by creating Him in our own image. He becomes, though we are unconscious of it, our self-appointed guarantor for all our own little " isms " about nature, and nations and race. Nor is it that the " secular " becomes the Hub of life instead. God remains at the hub and all our secular plans become blueprints ground into the dust beneath the ongoing inexorable wheel of truth. If sometimes, haphazard, we get beyond the blueprint to a construction, in no time that construction gets broken in the spokes.

3

This is what happens to us, corporately and personally, when there is no longer any such thing as a " Christian West." To play around on the fringe of chaos, booming out phrases that only had content in a bygone ordered age, only adds to man's frustrations.

For consider. Now that " awakened man " circles the globe and not just the borders of the Mediterranean, it is useless to expect the world to respond to the old controls. It is, for instance, high hypocrisy to cry of Africa and Asia " if only they were Christian." To them the very word spells something different from what it does to us. The rapid growth of the " Christian West's " standard of living is recognisably due to our exploitation of the East. This is not to say the great Empire builders, from all the Christian countries, were personally brutes or brigands. Usually men of high personal integrity, they were, for centuries, no more than representatives of us all in the common determination of the West to get on with life, while putting God on the fringe. In the impenetrable mystery that is God's plan, He seems, in this regard, to have allowed some wheat to grow amidst the tares. In amongst the tares of our exploitation, just sufficient missionary wheat has been sown to educate the African mind and awaken the Asian soul. If we now complain that by its growing turbulence the East is biting the hand that fed it, we must also admit how much of the chaff of exploitation we have mixed with these tiny grains of wheat.

The Lazarus East has sat long enough on the doorstep of the Dives West, while the West has given the East what was left over of our sumptuous faring. If the East now demands a comparable paradise, and the West faces with open eyes its damnation, it will be no more use, than in the parable, for the West at this late hour to go " personally religious " with offers of personal resurrection. If the West hear not Moses and the Prophets (whose word was the word of corporate salvation), neither will the West be saved " though one should rise from the dead " (individual salvation). The East is going to have its good time. The West is doomed unless God is recognised at the hub of all life, East and West.

GOD AT THE HUB AGAIN. AND HOW?

The reader may at this point suppose the argument will develop towards the recovery of a central authority in the name of God. A Roman Catholic reader, indeed, might be muttering, " the author is coming our way." And, to be truthful, a great many, outside Rome, but in the leadership of Western affairs, can be found, consciously or unconsciously, to be backing the Vatican in the hope of recovering a Christian authority over against Russia. But our God is a God that moves. In effect a central authority would be a reversion out of step with our times. Two factors make such a recovery impossible. The first factor is the point at which we have arrived in the historic process ; the second is the resulting makeup of modern Western Man.

THE POINT AT WHICH WE HAVE ARRIVED IN THE HISTORIC PROCESS

This can be most shortly envisaged in a familiar simile, which serves so long ·as we do not attach any great mystic content to it. It is the claim that our Christian civilisation is about to come of age : approaching its " twenty-first " century. It was a German philosopher who claimed that all development could be analysed in terms of thesis, antithesis and synthesis. The idea is not difficult if you apply it to the development of a normal young man. For roughly his first fourteen years he is tied to his mother's apron strings. He accepts her thesis about life. Proverbially, because normally, with adolescence anti-thesis sets in. He becomes difficult and opposes many of the theses he used to accept from mother. Around nineteen he can become very difficult indeed. But things begin to be different when he comes of age : a stabilised person, he adjusts the experiences he came to during anti-thesis to the theses of his childhood. He becomes Mr. Syn-thesis.

By our simile, the first fourteen centuries of Christian

5

civilisation were thesis. Mother Church taught men how to think and what to do. Around the fourteenth century Christian man broke away from his mother's apron strings. Anti-thesis set in. It became most difficult around the nineteenth century. Christian man went wild. He forgot the word " companion " which means the sharer of the loaf. " Each man for himself and the devil take the hindmost " was the personal rule of the road. This disease of independence also affected the conduct of the autonomous sovereign states that now were Europe. " Each Empire for itself and the devil take the hindmost " was, for instance, the rule of our road in Africa. Scan the map of that time and Africa resembles a very edible slab of good things from which the Christian West took bites: Dutch South Africa, British East Africa, German, French, Portuguese, Italian, Spanish Africa—the largest nations taking several bites. (No wonder Jesus gave His cross to an African to carry.) Such was the century of Anti-thesis, of independent man. The theory, more terribly than we yet admit, invaded even the understanding of our faith. It was then supremely that " Christianity " became an individual affair. It became simply a matter of each soul for itself and the devil take the toiling masses of Glasgow, of Paris and Berlin. Look through the hymn book and note the preponderance of individualistic hymns, all the most familiar bearing a nineteenth century date.

But God is still sovereign. He is at the hub. Everyone knows that synthesis is our need. It is only too clear now that " if it is each Empire for itself, the devil takes the lot." It is only too clear now that " if it is each man for himself the devil takes the lot." So nations plunge around towards synthesis; and so do men. Some would synthetise with socialist constructions, national and international. Others, shying at socialism, lest it " creep " towards materialism, pay lip service to freedom, but, to live, must plunge internationally at cartels or nationally at price rings and ever larger combines.

If the mark of the first fourteen centuries was dependence, the mark of the epoch now closing was independence. What the God of history now demands of us is interdependence: synthesis. This brings us to consider the other factor which prevents the recovery of a superimposed central authority. We cannot return to the vertical conception of unthinking dependence on an overarching authority. It is a horizontal conception by which we are challenged—the inter-relatedness of nations each with their sovereign claims. Indeed we are challenged by a factor even more serious: the sovereign claims of Western individualised man. It is this consciousness of being primarily individuals in our modern West, that creates the further complexity.

THE RESULTING MAKE UP OF MODERN MAN

The simple point here is that if you attempt to order Western democratic man, he just won't take it. An independent creature, isolated from any pattern, he may *intellectually* admit that only interdependence can now save us. But *emotionally* he still desires a continuance of nineteenth century independence. He will be " corralled " neither by ecclesiastical authority nor by civil. Take the Church and marriage. The Church can lay down its old dictates about the finality of the marriage vow, but the divorce rate continues much the same: scores of thousands a year, while only a hundred years ago they could be counted in tens. Or, in the civil sphere, take kingship. Right into modern history the idea of monarchy was unconsciously accepted. The Nation was instinctively accepted as " the King's people." The Georges were all very peculiar people, but the monarchy was taken for granted. Even Queen Victoria, we are apt to forget, was for the major part of her reign extremely unpopular, openly and constantly criticised by the press. Yet no one of consequence ever questioned the monarchy. The Nation was " the Queen's people." Personally, if only because I have lived some years of my life in Republics, I am not only a monarchist but an ardent one. But do not let us delude ourselves with the idea that we are, in the old understanding, the Queen's people. The remarkable—

7

and heartening—significance of the last Coronation was that there was crowned " the people's Queen." She was probably the first monarch really to be crowned by the universal and conscious suffrage of the people.

We must be clear of what this break, from " instinctive authority " to the authority of common suffrage, betokens in the mood of modern man: in other realms than kingship. If, in the realm of kingship, democracy has won through to a self-conscious appreciation of its value, the same mood has not made such strides in the more important area of God's authority. To keep the issue simple, take a modern Senior Bible Class. Less than fifty years ago this was a comparatively easy undertaking. There was the " vertical " teaching, spoken down by the parson to a receptive group of youth. In Scotland, based probably on the Westminster Confession, the patterned word was declared, no questions were elicited, and the class was dismissed. Try the same method to-day. You may get the appearance of acceptance but, if you are an earnest teacher, you will be horrified by the lacklustre of those accepting eyes. The children of modernity just won't take it. It must be argued out. They must be individually convinced. Just as there used to be, that is, the unconscious acceptance of " the nation's King " so there used to be the acceptance of the National Theology, Calvinist or Lutheran, or the Thirty-Nine Articles. Now, just as we have " the people's Queen " by common suffrage, there is no way through but the long one of recreating consciously in every soul a desire for the recrowning of our sovereign God, over all aspects of life.

Men are far from doing that yet. And the real crisis of our time is that, while that is now the only way through, all the complex terrifying issues of our modern day have to be decided by the universal suffrage now democratically granted to this half baked man !

No wonder independent, isolated man, intellectually aware of the crisis but emotionally leaderless and desirous of continuing independence, escapes to digging allotments or directing dominoes. No wonder the total vote falls two millions at a general election.

No wonder authoritarianism, communist or fascist, lurks around the political scene in France and Italy.

No wonder that, even in the quintessential democracy that is the United States, authoritarian legislation begins to slip through Congress.

No wonder Protestant clergy on the Continent, and recognisably at home, lose patience with the responsibilities that God has laid on each man's shoulders and attempt a new authoritarian pattern for our Faith, a " this or that which must be accepted or else get out."

No wonder fundamentalist evangelists have their day again, across America and coming into Europe, offering a facile personal salvation at the drop of a handkerchief, without the burden of thinking all things out. (And as a result no wonder that universally such evangelists re-iterate " no comment " on every burning issue of the day.)

No wonder the sociologists of the Roman Church (who have never accepted democracy—because they cannot) rub their hands in expectation as they envisage their own dream coming true, a mass reversion to a dependent faith : because they see the Protestant Church without a pattern, whole peoples without obedience, democracy without a faith.

*   *   *   *

We have attempted to cover a lot of ground. We started with the Theologian and the Politician over against one another ; we traced the cause in the declension from a Christian society : we have argued the impossibility of a return to a Christian society by the recovery of authoritarian means, and we have attempted to envisage the pretty pass in which we find ourselves. However fantastically foreshortened, it nonetheless seemed necessary.

It is only against some such background that folk may see how important is the recovery of a responsible democracy,

B   9

in what danger it stands, and how important it is for Christians to be involved again—both for the continuance of democracy and also for the recovery of the full proportions of our faith.

We can now afford to be a little more contemporaneous.

IS DEMOCRACY SO STABLE ?

It would be a good thing, in the first place, not to take parliamentary democracy quite so much for granted. It is a very recent growth. It is well within the memory of living man that universal suffrage has been granted in any land. It is also a comparatively small experiment in Government, if you reckon up the democracies with anything approaching universal suffrage. We must also face the fact that it covers a smaller area of the world than fifty years ago.

But there are more serious considerations. Have you considered the real threat to democracy as it is ? No, it does not come from Russia. The real threat is inherent in the nature of parliamentary democracy. Karl Marx, who wrote such nonsense about the nature of our world and the destiny of man, had nonetheless certain criticisms of parliamentary democracy we still might seriously review. Arthur Koestler, the ex-communist, in *The Yogi and the Commissar*, paraphrased this criticism, in effect, as follows :—

Parliamentary democracy has so far only functioned when the issues that divide the parties are *political* and not economic : concerned with the pace toward an agreed objective and not with the nature of the objective. When, however, the nature of the economic structure divides the parties, there are only two realist choices ; become a commissar, dictate a permanent economic direction and lift these issues from the dangers of general elections—in other words, create dictatorship. OR, if you don't like the word, and like less concentration camps and restrictions on freedom, etc., then be realist. Don't delude yourself that democracy will ever achieve a new economic line. No holders of economic power have ever pulled out without a fight. If you don't like dictatorship desist from political interest, go to your digging or dominoes, escape the unequal contest—become a Yogi. In some such terms Koestler para-phrased Marx.

Before you raise your eyebrows at such a conclusion, realise that, historically, parliamentary democracy has in fact, so far, only fruitfully worked where the issues have been political and not economic. In the stable nineteenth century, into the twentieth, there was in every democratic land a common economic objective. Towards it there worked, in opposition to each other, those with radical views, over against those with conservative views, of progress. Thus, every five years or so, alternating parties radically quickened the pace or con-servatively conserved the gains. It worked well because the division was political. There was fundamental acceptance of the economic objective. But the moment the differing con-victions are not about the pace towards a common objective, but about the very nature of the objective, the whole process is in jeopardy. To over-simplify and make the point, the moment one side is set for economic planning and the other for economic freedom the real crisis of parliamentary democracy begins. The engine begins to seize up, for instance, if you nationalise for five years and then denationalise after the next election! This is essentially the claim of Marx: once you perceive the issue is economic, it is " romantic " to suppose you will get progress by pretending to be nice to each other. You must lay down one economic line and stick to it, requiring a dictatorship to make permanent the line.

Had this been just theory, it need have no place here. But is this not what is happening in Europe? Take France. Why is she politically decrepit? It is difficult, of course, to write of France—kaleidoscopic in its changes. Yet it is in the ongoing situation that God speaks and we must endeavour to trace His ceaseless writing on the wall. The message is essentially the same. Two elections ago the thesis was clearest: two parties, with about a hundred members each, were represented by the Communists and the de Gaullists on either extreme.

Each group had an economic theory it would stabilise. Each said honestly enough that if power came their way they would suspend parliamentary democracy to make permanent their version of the Corporate State. Pressured between them there were some four hundred democratic members, split into no less than eleven parties, the largest of which commanded less members than either non-parliamentary extreme. There you could see parliamentary democracy ceasing to function. Indeed, two Parliaments ago, they devised a law of representation to make almost impossible a government of either extreme. Had this happened in Russia, it would have been called by us " trimming the elections." In the 1956 Elections it does not look so neat, but the issue is the same. The anti-parliamentary Communist Left now hold 150 seats. If on the extreme Right the Poujadistes have ousted the de Gaullists, they still, with 50 seats, represent the anti-Parliamentary pattern, and are already in league with the reactionary forces in French Africa, who openly scorn what Parliament decides. Poujade was a leader in the fascist Petain Youth Movement during the war. One-third of the present Parliament are against parliamentary democracy and between the two extremes there jostle, impotent, some ten democratic parties unable to achieve a viable demarcation between democratic right and left. The ominous pattern stands. In Italy they recently promulgated a similar law, faced with the same central problem. In both countries millions of adults vote for the two extremes : and, between them, parliamentary democracy is almost pressured to death. It is more obvious on the Continent because the French are logical and the Italians are poor.

The pattern is not yet apparent in Britain because we have never been logical and, comparatively, we are not yet poor. We still have parliamentary democracy and the suffrage is roughly fifty-fifty between the radical mood and the conservative. But who would deny that politics are in danger of getting more bitter ? This is because the real issue, despite verbal evasions on both sides, is Planning versus Freedom.

Now, taken in the large, nothing is more certain than that any nation that is to survive in our interlaced world must move towards planning. This is not simply a party political statement. Bernard Shaw once said that the greatest delusion of the British public was that they had read *The Origin of Species*! If more had actually done so we would not have such nonsense talked about " the survival of the fittest." The phrase does not mean the survival of the beefiest. It means almost the direct opposite : that only those forms of life survive that are inherently capable of coming level with a new environment. Our age must be one of interdependence, between classes, between nations, between East and West. Any nation that does not ultimately come level with this our environment will perish. Both Parties show signs of coming level : that is why it is not a party political statement. Americans are fond of referring to socialism as " creeping," fearing it must creep into communism. What they do not realise is that this is the direction in which it *will* creep unless the Planning concept is kept within parliamentary democracy. What they also do not realise is that conservatism is also creeping—towards planning! " You are all socialists now " would be the comment of any nineteenth century Tory who came into our midst. In the acceptance of these two realisations lies our hope.

The continuance of parliamentary democracy depends on the ability of both Parties to come level with our inevitable environment, without revolution ; or, more exactly, the ability voluntarily to get under " the planning umbrella " on both sides of the House. Then there would be a chance of one side going radically at it, and the other conservatively, with a new common objective. Should that happen, Marx is defeated at his strongest point.

There is, of course, a facile optimism abroad that it has happened. " Both parties are planners now " . . . " Very little separates them " . . . and so on. But a little more realism would be healthy. Granted continuing economic prosperity we might so scrape along. But assume widespread unemployment and would there not arise, overnight, the ugliest catcalls from Left and Right ? Our world is so interdependent that a recession anywhere might rapidly affect the whole. America plans for ever growing prosperity. The same catchphrases invade our own propaganda. But can this permanently be a mark of the West while the millions in the East can never adequately be integrated with such a Western economy ? Is there not danger of a log jam when the burden of increasing Western prosperity becomes confluent with the rightful demands of the East ? A recession anywhere might jam the lot. Then would folk be so complacent ? It is well to be forearmed.

Most recently, again, there is even an international optimism. " Geneva " lulls the mind. Peace may indeed have broken out, born of the universal recognition that modern war might effect nothing but the extermination of mankind. But it is well to be forearmed here too. " Peace " could have disturbing consequences. It is not just that our prosperity is largely geared to war preparation, and that relaxed tension might lead to unemployment. It is also that the economic prosperity of the West is largely maintained by vast American investment in France and Italy. American isolationists have only been kept from stopping this investment by their fear of Russia. Take away that fear and the Europe that lies between might in no time be thrown back on its own resources. They then would find how tenuous their own resources are, with a self-sufficient America on one hand and a faster moving Russian economy, released from war expenditure, on the other. The Russian form of dictatorship, shorn of its " bogy man " apparel, would be the more enticing to the citizens in the crippled democracies of Italy and France.* European parliamentary democracy, with its comparably slow and shuffling gait, might the quicker be in jeopardy in an era of universal peace! The challenge still stands—Freedom or Planning. So let us look now at Democracy in modern times.

---

*In the 1956 French Election the Communists increased their vote by almost 500,000 conceivably for this reason.

WHO ARE THE LEFT ?

Consider, for a moment, the meaning of " The Left "—an interesting label. It stems from a Council Chamber designed as a horseshoe, faced by the chairman (or Mr. Speaker). From ancient days the *status quo* was the right arm of the Chairman : " the King's men "—the Right side of the horseshoe. The pace was made by the opposition—precisely, the Left. (" Philosophers " sat, as they always do, on the cross benches facing the chair !) All through history the Left is seen as the Demon King. " If he gets power the world will come to an end." In recent history Shaftesbury, Gladstone, Lloyd George, Ramsay MacDonald, all had this said of them. Yet through history such men have made the pace-bringing legislation level with the new environment. They have concocted the new recipe, to keep legislation fit for the new environment, which the *status quo* party finally swallow with a grimace—usually later claiming the recipe as the elixir which they were considering all along !

The Demon King to-day is, of course, Bevan. His regrettable expletives should not blind us to his significance. For what is happening ? The official Labour leadership, lulled or enlightened as you will, more and more play in with the Right (" there is no difference between the parties "). But massing behind the old Labour leaders there grows up in new formation, the turbulent " new Left." Now it is shortsighted to wish it did not exist. For the moment there is no recognisable and radical Left, parliamentary democracy is in danger. It means there are no really new ideas coming up. The measure of passion created by Bevan is really the measure of men's laziness, their desire to stay put. If this desire is not permanently challenged from the Left, there arises the danger of lassitude in popular Government. The issue is far broader and more serious than the personality of a man. But if, with our modern propaganda, and with our international interdependence, men perpetually build up Bevan (or whoever takes his essential place) as a wrecker; and if, on the real Left taking power, there is a flight from the pound, and real political bitterness, then the responsibility would lie as much with the many who forget the changing environment and the true health of democracy as with those they blame. But if that thought is designed as a brickbat in one direction, it is right to throw one also at the extreme Left. They in their turn are shortsighted if they try to rally the new Left with outdated cries of " bloated capitalists and double crossers." This is not only bad psychology but quite untrue. Such outworn cries constantly fog the vital contribution that a responsible new radical Left has to make. Bevan's biggest mistake is the fogging of his real insights by those old bitter speeches, which may have had content in the thirties, but make even Labour blush in the fifties, and which he yet continues to deliver. But the persistence with which the popular press headline his gaffes and have not room to report his constructions is also the measure of their fear of what a constructive radical Left is really saying. Essentially it claims that you cannot solve the problems of our domestic economy domestically: we are interlaced with the world. And it is for this we must be planned. It isn't just that County Councils cannot move without Whitehall. It is that the Board of Trade cannot move without the United Nations and constant International Conference. It is years ago that Bevan said our rearmament commitments would cripple us, and the newspaper files of the time are worth review for their scorning of his case. Four years later Winston Churchill admitted Bevan was right. Again, in season and out, Bevan has persisted that for America and the West to build up Western Germany must mean war. Please God a new *detente* may prevent that. But if the problem of German unity is solved, the outline of the solution will be consonant with his case from the start. Again, at the Geneva Conference, the press blazoned the brilliant suggestions of the premier of France. He proposed an international organisation to control funds, set free by reduction of armaments, that they might be diverted to economic aid to underdeveloped countries. Surely every heart beats faster at the mere possibility that such might happen. Every mind knows that this would be a real turning from darkness to light. We would not only be saved the economic chaos that threatens from radical disarmament, in a world geared for war. The vast sums ear-marked for destruction would be applied to construction, creating ultimately immense new Eastern markets for the now constructive, re-employment of the West. What a moving suggestion, compact alike of true charity and prudence. It is now four years since Bevan made the same suggestion! I have counted it wise to be a little detailed in these last sentences, so saturated is the general belief, among most Church readers, that the radical Left is " wild man madness," when the respon-sible acceptance of its right to exist is in fact an essential safeguard of healthy democracy. The issue is broader and more serious than the personality of a man.

THE REAL ISSUE

That said, we come to the apex of our analysis. It is not true, we have said, that in our internal economy bloated capitalists are the trouble. The cartoonists' picture of a corpu-lent gentleman, with white waistcoat, gold watch chain and top-hat, is out of date, in our internal economy. *The real issue in our interdependent world is this: it is the whole West that may well, and quite unconsciously as yet, be fulfilling that role.* If you like to put it so, the business man and coster, the trade unionist and parson, Tom, Dick, Harry, you and I are sporting a sort of collective white waistcoat and top hat. All together—the whole citizenry of U.S.A. and Europe may well turn out to be a primary cause of the world's trouble. Marx prophesied that the rich would get richer and the poor poorer till the latter turned and rent the waistcoat, smashed the hat and pinched the watch. We now laugh at Marx because it has not happened. Tom, Dick and Harry have waistcoats enough, and watches, to yawn at the old cartoons. There is no proletariat left to rise, in Britain or the United States.

But what if we have " exported our proletariat ? " What if

Africa and South-East Asia now, by their ill-paid sweat, make rich the Western world ? Are we so certain that they will never rise ? The answer is summed up in the comment of a business magnate to me in South Africa :—" If I was an African I would be a communist ! "

It is Africa and South-East Asia, with the added burden of increasing population, that are becoming poorer and poorer. Yet indeed they keep the Western economy alive. For again consider. Most folk now know the importance of keeping the dollar gap closed. Our whole British standard of living, our ability to " maintain the ministry," the keeping of our people in a " State of Welfare," our pensions schemes ; all, in short, that keeps Britain stable, is dependent on keeping closed that gap. And how have we done it ? Not the least factor is that, since 1945, our colonies in Africa and Malaya alone have paid up a thousand million pounds to keep *our* dollar gap closed ! But for our colonies, the economy of Britain would have collapsed after the war with similarly appalling social consequences as attended the economic collapse of Germany.*

That is just a factual glimpse of how interlaced is our world, how morally bound we are to see the real problem of our time as not domestic but global, and how " planning " is not just a political catch phrase but a necessity of prudence and, for a Christian, an obligation of obedience. If we do not plan more quickly and more fairly, Africa will rise, not because it is barbaric, but by the direct act of the living God. But the moment we are back to planning we are in the arena of party politics again, at its most difficult and explosive point.

CHURCHMEN MUST BE INVOLVED

Since we dared to become contemporaneous we have covered a deal of ground. We have seen that even domestically democracy is not something you can take for granted. We have

---

*Economists tell me that all this will one day come back to them through London. But there are enough educated Africans now to ask whether it is not in fact a Kathleen Mavourneen loan ; it may be for years and it may be forever !

seen the significance of a realist Left as essential both to progress and vital democracy. We have seen the real issue as global and moral. And earlier we saw that, if democracy is to continue, the solution of these problems lies in the brittle hands of half-baked modern man : intellectually aware that interdependence is our obligation, emotionally still desirous to retain his independence.

If Western civilisation is to win through, without revolution, the qualities of vision, tolerance, patience are in demand as they have not been for centuries. By all means let us retain the phrase that we must " outlive and outlove the Communists," but let us be a little more aware of the cost of such an ideal. It is here that Christians have a peculiar part to play. So much have we made a " hobby " of God and a " department " of religion, that we forget that this is part of what, contemporaneously, *Pentecost* is about. " All nations " are gathered now, not just in the street outside an Upper Room, but in the Main Street of the world. Only Galileans have the word that can equally be understood in all languages. And it is no less than the whole world that must move towards an understanding of the meaning—for our day—of " all things in common." This is the " environment " to which God is directing our world. Any nation that shrinks from it, in that measure threatens its own survival. The plea is not Utopian. I have not fallen for those who simplify, saying that the West are the " Haves " and the East the " Have nots " and that if the West " gave away " the problem would be squared. On the contrary, it seems proved that if available purchasing power were shared out now it would make the fairly well off nations very poor and leave the very poor nearly as they were. Far less am I hinting, as I have already argued, that it is for the rich as individuals to take action. In Great Britain in 1938 there were 6,560 people with an annual income of over £6,000 after paying income tax. In the year 1953/4 only 35 persons were in that position.* But I am arguing that something explosive

*Quoted from *Money* by E. Rogers : Edinburgh House Press.

is in our midst when half the population of the world get 9 per cent of the world's income. And the more we admit there is not enough food produced in the world to give everyone an adequate diet, the more inexcusable becomes the high proportion that all the western nations subscribe to the cost of goods so unproductive as armaments.

I am arguing that every Christian must be involved when we face the facts that a baby girl born in Canada can expect to live to the age of 69 : born in India, the expectation is only 27 years ; or that in Sweden infant deaths are 31.1 out of every thousand births, and in Gambia 369.

I am arguing, as a Galilean, that there is only one way left : if the East is going to listen to the West, and the West is to continue to speak of Christian solutions. That way is planning. And world planning involves national planning.

Personally I am a socialist. I do not mention this assuming that anyone is particularly interested in the fact, but to make clear that if anything is to be done beyond resounding slogans then it can only be done through Parliament, and by men taking sides. I am a socialist because for them planning comes first and freedom finds its place within it. If freedom means "doing as you please," then the free man is he who drives his car across a *zebra* crossing when pedestrians are using it ; or, at the other extreme, the quintessence of a free man was Hitler. But if freedom is "the liberty to do as you ought" then freedom has nothing ultimately to fear from the planners.

But that last pregnant sentence has a twin issue. Firstly, if freedom be defined as "the liberty to do as you ought," Christians are peculiarly needed in political affairs. We have earlier argued that the future of our world is now in the hands of half-baked, confused democractic man. Very few of them would so think of freedom. If the word is to be saved from prostitution in conservative ranks and to be responsibly recovered in socialist ranks, there is an urgent need in the policy making committees of both sides for those who can give content to the word "ought," and who have a living faith that "ought" is capable of translation into "can." Only committed and involved Christians can be trusted to incarnate these contentions, and save both parties from the disasters of expediency.

But secondly, and related, such is the self-centredness of man (sin is the old word) that planning can go just as far agley as freedom. While the drive must be toward planning, such is the complacency of sinful man that if planning got the saddle without constant opposition it would land in that impoverished mass of shortcuts and bedevilments that is correctly called secularism.

By and large, I suppose our choices of Conservatism or Socialism are due at least as much to our psychological make ups as to any cold evaluation of the political problems concerned. There just are radical types and conservative types. And just as the ideal dual partnership in a business is an ebullient man and a canny, so we have in Britain an ideal Constitution if we continue to use it with vision and candour. However annoying the freedom men are to the ardent socialists, and indeed however often they fall for less worthy interpretations of freedom (fall, that is, for *their* secularism), they can fulfil the function, consciously or otherwise, of checking the sin that lurks in every plan that falls short of God's plan.

Provided an overriding admission that we must move toward planning to come level with our world, how essential are two sides forever to that horseshoe: the pace-makers and the restrainers; alternatively in power.

For let us not forget that this is precisely the genius of our Constitution. Britain is never, in fact, governed by Labour or by Conservatives. Britain is governed by the Houses of Parliament. The Prime Minister is a salaried official of the State. But the Leader of the Opposition is also salaried. He is, correctly, the Leader of *Her Majesty's Opposition*.

We have in our *Constitution*, that is, the only way of going Left.

To degenerate into a dictatorship, either violently, or more subtly by the gradual absence of a realist opposition, is always a latent danger. But dictatorship is no way of going Left. When Power is not limited by effective criticism its greatest danger is its false assumption that it retains its ideals. It never renounces justice or freedom. It merely, and sometimes quite sincerely, postpones their application. In so doing it forgets a living God; forgets that during the period of suspension sinister forces accumulate, creating new situations which in face make impossible the reintroduction of justice and freedom. Thus, dictatorship is no way of going Left. It is a certain way of going in circles.

So we come to our conclusions :—

(a) If we are to survive we must plan internationally.

(b) This is meaningless unless we plan nationally.

(c) Such is man's sin that the controllers must be controlled.

(d) Our Constitution is the finest instrument yet devised, in a wicked world, to " plan for freedom."

While these sound the merest cliches, if you examine them you find that only Christian insights will carry them through. Yet churchmen are not in the forefront of policy making in either of the main parties. This is not a gratuitous insult. Large numbers of politicians go to church. But religion has become, for them as for us, a department of their private lives. Indeed the more hard-baked the politician the more you can expect, on the rare occasions when he refers to the faith, that he will say " for my part I take my stand on the Sermon on the Mount." Now of all the statements in the Bible that seem incapable of translation into terms of political realism in the twentieth century I would commend the Sermon on the Mount. Not only, then, has something gone wrong with our understanding of the significance of politics, but something has gone wrong with our understanding of the significance of the Bible.

This book is designed to put both these wrongs a little more right. Only then can we hope to bring the theologian and the politician of the opening paragraph of this chapter closer together.

CHAPTER TWO

THERE IS ONE WAY LEFT FOR THE CHURCH

This second chapter is briefer. The main body of the book is concerned with the causes for churchmen's indifference to politics; and with an outline of how a recovery can be made. We can therefore confine the chapter to two introductory questions. Firstly, should the kind of issues raised in the first chapter find place in a religious book at all? Secondly, even supposing political issues are an outreach of the Gospel, is not the task of the Church to confine itself to the Gospel?

WAS IT A STRANGE OPENING FOR A RELIGIOUS BOOK?

I wrote: " Religion has become the hobby of the few. If a man likes music he goes to the conservatoire. If painting, he seeks out an artist's studio. Or, if certain psychic elements predominate in his make-up he ' takes up ' God. The real trouble is that the Bible is not about that sort of religion at all. In the Bible God is a total sovereign, not a personal solace. Authentic solace resides in a serious acceptance of His total sovereignty." If you counter that claim then I must " reserve my defence " for development in the chapters that follow. What I would here make clear is the extent to which, consciously or unconsciously, churchmen do counter it.

I was recently in the United States—the very first country in which, let me say at once, I would seek citizenship were I ever denied it here. But what frightened me was the main trend of Protestant religion: that the purpose of the Faith is to adjust a person to life as it is. The archpriest of this approach, a most sincere man, writes books that exceed two million copies in circulation. His packed church carries, in its weekday staff, three full time psychiatrists. No one can scorn him. If there are that many people maladjusted, and if far vaster numbers are so ill at ease with themselves that " peace " is what they seek from the pulpit, then it is religion's place to provide for the spiritually down-and-out as much as, in times of depression, it should cater for the physically down-and-out. But what is he to preach? Is the Bible's main purpose to adjust a man to the world as it is? Is not peace rather found in a commitment to adjust the world to God's purpose? " Thy Kingdom come, Thy will be done, on earth as it is in Heaven " is the first petition Our Lord asked us to make after the adoration of God's Name. If indeed our world in God's purpose, be a brotherhood—a companionship, a sharing of the loaf—and if we ponder such figures as we have earlier quoted of the gross disparity existing between East and West—have we any right to peace? Jeremiah hears God inveighing against the covetousness of His chosen people and has grim words to communicate to His priests, " They have healed also the hurt of my people lightly, saying, ' Peace, peace; when there is no peace '." And if in impatience folk say, " but these are vast issues and surely we are entitled to personal peace," the Word of God goes immediately on— " ask for the old paths where is the good way, and walk therein, *and ye shall find rest for your souls.*" Nor is there any doubt from the context that the old paths were the way of social righteousness. What has gone wrong in American religion is the terrible cleavage between Church activity—never more prosperous than to-day—and any realistic sense of God's sovereignty in history and His demands upon us in His now unified world. " Trust ye not in lying words," goes on Jeremiah, " saying the Temple of the Lord, the Temple of the Lord, the Temple of the Lord, are these. For if ye thoroughly amend your ways and your doings; if ye thoroughly execute judgment between a man and his neighbour; if ye oppress not the stranger, the fatherless, and the widow . . . neither walk after other gods to your hurt: then will I cause you to dwell in this place . . . "*

*The passages quoted are from *Jeremiah* : chapters 6 and 8. Nor can we escape the parallel to America's great fear as it is recorded in the 6th chapter, " Thus said the Lord, behold a people cometh from the north country;

At a recent conference, where I developed the relationship of social justice to personal peace, an elderly lady came to me with tears in her eyes. " You upset completely the old satisfying religion my father taught me," she complained. It is not a pleasant experience to upset anybody and I longed for a word of comfort that would not betray The Word. But I was tongue-tied. Her father was indeed an earnest Christian, who had been in Shanghai. That very afternoon I had read of an advertisement that had appeared some years ago, before the Revolution, in one of the Shanghai papers. It was issued by one of the great mills for the purpose of inducing additional investment in its stock. Here was the advertisement† :—

" The profits of the ——————— factory surpassed $1,000,000. For the past two years it has been running night and day with scarcely any intermission. The number of hands employed is 2,500, and the following is the wage table per day :—

Men—15 to 20 cents ; boys above 15 years—10 to 15 cents ; girls above 15 years—5 to 10 cents ; small boys, and boys and girls under 10 years—from 3½ to 10 cents.

The working hours are from five-thirty in the morning until five-thirty in the evening, and from five-thirty in the evening until five-thirty in the morning. No meals are supplied by the factory.

It will be seen that the company is in an exceptionally favourable position with an abundant supply of cheap labour to draw from. The annual profits have exceeded the total capital on at least three occasions."

---

and a great nation shall be stirred up from the uttermost parts of the earth. They lay hold of bow and spear ; they are cruel and have no mercy ; their voice roareth as the sea and they ride upon horses ; everyone set in array, as a man to the battle, against thee, O daughter of Zion. We have heard the fame thereof : our hands wax feeble ; anguish hath taken hold of us, and pangs as a woman in travail . . . ''

†Quoted from *Are Foreign Missions Done For?* by Robert Speer.

When I say the father was an earnest Christian I sincerely mean it. But I could not help wondering if it ever occurred to him that such an advertisement was proper subject of protest by a Christian; if he did not suppose that " the important thing was to preach the Gospel first." I could not help wondering whether, had I worked as a child in that factory, I would in manhood have been very depressed when the Communists came along offering a New Day, or very impressed by the pleas from the West to fight instead for the freedom I had enjoyed under democracy.

All this flashed through my mind as that elderly lady cried on my arm. I was tongue-tied. Where on earth could one " begin " ?

I am blaming no one. I could easily have been in Shanghai when that advertisement appeared and I have always considered myself an earnest Christian. I am near as anything certain that it would not have occurred to me to protest either. Barring a thin red line of Christian protesters in the last three centuries (who have all in their day been written off as a lunatic fringe with such comment as " It's a pity he has deserted the central message for some social bee in his bonnet ") the Church simply has not made the nexus. It has concerned itself with " getting the Gospel right first." Thus we are where we are : with a unified world toppling on the edge of chaos for lack of the Galilean Word that alone can bring the next approximation to Justice. While the Church gnaws at its fingers in mystification that the vast majority in East and West pass us by as irrelevant : except as magic guardians of everlasting life, in which they are not particularly interested unless certain psychic elements predominate in their make up.

Really to restore the peace of that elderly lady I would have had to embark on the whole thesis of this book, which would have been tedious for both of us as she held my arm.

But perhaps I do not carry you with me. " The Faith is transcendent, politics are of the earth," you protest. If that be your conviction then three things must be said. In the first

26

place—perhaps to your surprise—you have fallen for Communist Russia's view of Religion. Precisely do they believe that the whole area of politics and economics is an autonomous realm, with its own sufficient rules. For those who want their souls to be " processed " in addition, Russia is willing enough to leave some churches open. But woe betide the priest who crosses the line and makes comment on the things of earth! With these you " companion," sharing some heavenly bread as a foretaste of some banquet hereafter.

In the second place, and by corollary, you must not be surprised if politics degenerate into all the bedevilments of secularism. For it is just there that you have joined with the Communists in placing them.

In the third place, I shall be very surprised if you are still reading your Bible *as a Bible*. You may still be devoted to the psalms, passing by as irrelevant that the very lifeblood of David was politics, and thus bypassing often enough the essence of their meaning. You may still be searching the Gospels, concentrating, as the years go by, on smaller and smaller portions as alone bearing fruit in personal solace. But the great sweep of the rest—of the Law, of the Prophets, of the forces that had to be rid of Christ before His ministry got going, of the Revelation of the Last Things—all this somehow you will have laid aside as " too high for us, we cannot attain unto them."

Such is the final destination of those who make the neat division that " Religion is transcendent, politics are of the earth." And it is because so many approximate to that destination that this book is attempted.

I would claim that if the Law-Givers and the Prophets came back, the Apostles and the early Church, they would not count the opening chapter strange for a religious book. All through the Bible the contemporary situation is the arena in which you meet God.   .

27

BUT EVEN SUPPOSING POLITICAL ISSUES ARE AN OUTREACH, IS NOT
THE TASK OF THE CHURCH TO CONFINE ITSELF TO THE GOSPEL ?

Again the main answer to this is developed in the following
chapters. But this can be said here—the book is designed for
churchmen, for those who *have* closed with the Gospel.
Perhaps it is true there are few *strict* pietists left ; such as
would maintain that our isolated Christian obligation is to
develop our interior souls. What concerns me is the large
number who, admitting social obligation, in fact stand short
of implementing it. " Once a man has the Gospel," they
argue, " he can be trusted to get involved." But does this
work out in practice ? Are churchmen in the forefront of
truly visionary political involvement ? Three years ago we
organised a meeting for " War on Want " to focus our obligation to the under-developed countries. A churchman was
in the chair. The two main speakers were a Labour and a
Conservative member of parliament. Clergy everywhere
co-operated in advertising the meeting ; the Trade Unions
were more chary of being officially involved. Four hundred
churches were invited to send delegates : and about twenty
Trade Union branches. And at the meeting ? About sixty
persons from the churches and about two hundred from the
Trade Unions ! " Once a man has the Gospel " can he be
trusted to be involved—even when both parties are on the
platform ? " Ah ! " says someone, " but the trouble with
churchmen is that most of them have never been properly
converted." I personally do not like that language. But I
regret to have to report that it is precisely those congregations
who use that language who are the most difficult of all to corral
to a meeting of such practical intent. They are forever organ-
ising the next Revival campaign, so that more can " get Christ "
and so become involved, while they themselves who have
" got Christ " continue to escape involvement ! They might be
compared to the authoritarians, already noted in the last
chapter, who suspend freedom assuming it can be restored
any time, oblivious of the bedevilments that occur during the

suspension, which in cumulation prevent the restoration. Similarly, those most sincere evangelists, e.g., in pre-Revolution Shanghai, suspend immediate attack on social injustice " to declare the Gospel first," oblivious of the inexorable march of events which bring in the Communists instead. Just as the Authoritarians, intending to move left, in fact end by moving in circles, so these good people end by revolving in " church circles " failing to affect the whole.

I like Dr. Phillips' paraphrase* of the Epistle to the Hebrews :

" Let us leave behind the elementary teaching about Christ and go forward to adult understanding. Let us not lay over and over again the foundation truths—repentance from the deeds which led to death, believing in God, baptism and laying on of hands, belief in the life to come and the final Judgment. *No, if God allows, let us go on.*"

Yet, lest any imagine *we* have dropped the Gospel and taken up instead some counterfeit alternative called social concern, it may be advisable to recall what the Gospel is. *What is the Gospel ?* It is the Bible's interpretation of why man is where he is : and of Man's way out. Man, claims the Bible, is not fatally determined by his economic circumstance, as the Communists would have it, nor by his chemical components, as the Behaviourists would have it : or by any of the " isms," or " wasms " by which, through history, philosophers have attempted to analyse his plight. Man, claims the Bible, is fatally determined by sin. This it declares not in a series of philosophical principles, but in a " movie " of consequent events. Creation is made good. Man, the apex of creation, is also made good. He starts off as God's co-operator in a Garden where everything is lovely. It is important that it is a Garden. True Nature, for the Bible, is not what we generally picture it : virgin soil before Man has had a hand in it. The story is relevant here of the somewhat pompous parson leaning over the gate with the farmer, viewing a fine crop of barley.

---

*Letters to the Younger Churches, J. B. Phillips. Hebrews, chapter 6.

"It is wonderful," said the parson, "what can be done when you and God get together." "Aye," said the farmer, "but you should have seen this field last year when God had it all to Himself." I hope the parson took the opportunity of explaining the Bible view of true nature. For the second scene in this consequent movie (*Genesis* 2) is of Man being created *before* the plants and herbs, declaring that the work of man in tillage is as essential as the rain for bringing into existence True Nature. God the eternal Worker (*John* 5, 17) created Man to be a worker (*Genesis* 2, 15). The purpose of creation and of Man is fulfilled when worker meets Worker in the fruit of their co-operation. Thus, further, as the type of true nature is not vegetation but a Garden, so the expression of spiritual fulfilment is not "the natural" (in modern thinking), nor even the cultivated wheat and vine, but Bread and Wine, products of Divine-human co-operation. In the next scene (*Genesis* 3), Man decides to run his own creation and his own production—his true nature gets broken. Man ceases to co-operate with God, gets broken from Him, and gets broken from nature. "Pride rules His will." And the sons of Adam, Cain and Abel, through a disastrous murder, convey both the glory and shame of Man: Cain both hating his brother and yet conscience-stricken about the lost brotherhood. Further the very earth gets soured in consequence of the Fall. Both creation and production get out of gear.

As Gerard Manley Hopkins has it in his *God's Grandeur*—

> *Generations have trod, have trod, have trod,*
> *And all is seared with trade: bleared, smeared with toil:*
> *And wears man's smudge and shares man's smell: the soil*
> *Is bare now, nor can foot feel, being shod.*

From then on, the Bible is a pageantry of Kings and Prophets and Priests, as deviating and complex as real life but converging in this: a determination, as glorious as it is pathetic, to bring all life back to God through Man: to re-establish the true nature of things, where all can cry "glory."

All I seek to convey here is that the Bible is not about an individual transaction between individual atomised men and their Maker, as if the earth were a neutral backcloth before which a drama is played. It is the story of a Creation and the break in that Creation. It is the story of Man, the gardener, who defied co-operation with His Maker, who can never forget what the Garden once looked like, who with one part of him seeks renewed co-operation, but with another part of him cannot resist " one more shot " at getting the place right by himself! This is what the pageant of Kings and Priests and Prophets is about—so full of herb offerings, and beast offerings, interspersed with animal lusts—in the Old Testament.

The New Testament is God's answer. " In the place where Jesus was crucified there was a Garden " (*John* 19, 41), " and in the Garden a new tomb." From that Tomb the New Man rose lifting from its bondage the whole body of things as well as of men. True Nature was re-established. Man in Christ is made the heir once more of a new earth. No wonder Mary, on the Resurrection morning, " thought He was the Gardener " : for indeed He was—the new Adam and the New Man ; the restored co-operation ; the at-one-ment again.

This cosmic significance of the Gospel has never quite been lost by the Church. It was a Celtic missionary of the 6th century who wrote, " Sing my tongue how glorious battle glorious victory became," and further he declares,

> *From His patient body pierced*
> *Blood and water streaming fall* :
> Earth and sea and stars and mankind
> *By that stream are cleansed all.*

And it was a 19th century Hymnist who wrote,

> *For well we know this* weary soiled earth
> *Is yet Thine own by right of* its new birth
> *Since that great Cross upreared on Calvary*
> *Redeemed it from its fault and shame to Thee.*

It is here by derivation, that politics, production, manufacture as well as man, are involved in the Good News. The whole vast pageantry of kings and priests and prophets that constitute the ongoing history of humanity are not the backstage chorus before whom the drama of each single man's salvation is played out with God. It is by involvement in and through the pageantry of ongoing life that our Salvation is wrought.

" Must I utterly renounce all the things about me," asked F. D. Maurice, " that I may be absorbed into Him, or is there any way in which I can devote them and myself to Him, and only know Him the better by filling my place among them ? "

BUT IS NOT THE GOSPEL PERSONAL ?

If you feel that is too " corporate," go to some text of St. Paul to which we now give " individual " content and it culminates in the same conclusion. The work of the Cross was never more closely summed than in the assertion of St. Paul that " God was in Christ, reconciling the world to Himself, not reckoning unto them their trespasses and having committed unto us the word of reconciliation." Here in three sentences is the catharsis of the Cross, the comfort of the Cross and the consequence of the Cross.

" God was in Christ reconciling the world unto Himself." A medical student once told me that from the age of seventeen till his graduation he hated his father, so much did he drive him to his studies. But on the night before the graduation his father explained that when the lad was seventeen his own doctor had warned him to give up business as he might drop dead. Without capital he decided to remain at business in the hope that he would survive till his boy's graduation; but he also ensured, by driving, that the boy would not have a delayed course. " From that moment," said the young medical, " I was reconciled to my father." Now, if we are to be honest, but for Christ's revelation of what God is really like, it would sometimes be hard to be reconciled to God. Time and again He does not seem to care for the individual. He seems a hard

Taskmaster. If He makes His sun to shine on the evil and the good He seems also at times as indiscriminate in the blows He distributes to the good as to the evil. I have never seen the problem of undeserved suffering satisfactorily answered. We can all understand the child who said " I love Jesus but I hate God." But if really to see Jesus is to see God then, by Faith if not by sight, we are indeed reconciled to God. We see the Truth of God behind " the seeming." No one can put into words the love of the Father, as Jesus reveals it. We can only fumble with inadequate human parallels, such as the love of a mother at her best. The love of a mother consists in going on loving you whatever you do to her. Le Poer Trench sums it in the lines:

> *A poor lad once and a lad so trim*
> *Gave his love to her who loved not him.*
> *And said she, " Bring me to-night, you rogue,*
> *Your mother's heart to feed my dog."*
>
> *To his mother's house went that young man,*
> *Killed her, cut out her heart and ran,*
> *But as he was running, look you, he fell*
> *And the heart rolled out on the ground as well.*
>
> *And the lad, as the heart was arolling, heard*
> *That the heart was speaking and this was the word—*
> *The heart was weeping and crying so small*
> *" Are you hurt, my child, are you hurt at all? "*

What Jesus reveals about God is indeed a catharsis; " a purification of the emotions by vicarious experience." God, it is revealed, does not concern Himself as to how far we hurt Him. We can proceed to crucify Him if we wish. What concerns God is how far we hurt ourselves in the process! Here is Love indeed.

" God was in Christ reconciling the world to Himself, not reckoning unto men their trespasses." What comfort without condition is here! Someone has compared it to the difference

33

between a minus sign and a plus. Psychologically, a minus
sign spells gloom. Let the housewife find a minus sign at the
end of her weekly account with the grocer, or the business
man find a minus sign at the end of the draft of his annual
balance sheet : there is gloom. But this has not reference only
to financial accounts. Who does not admit that the account
of his life so far is a minus sign ? " The good that I would I
do not, but the evil which I would not, that I do." That cry of
St. Paul is universal experience. What upsets every scene,
domestic or political, is not man's desire to be bad. So far
I have never met a man who wanted to be bad. The mystery
of man is that he is bad when he wants to be good. This is his
shame and his glory. This is his departure from his true nature
which makes him unable to co-operate with his Maker. This
is his share in the sin of Adam. On the third of September 1939—
when the Second Great War was declared—there were 400
million people in Europe. At least 398 million did not want
to go to war. So we went to war ! This is the mystery of man,
domestic and political. And it was with this that God came
to deal, through Christ, the New Man. What He did—in
the central scene of our consequent drama—was to come down
out of highest heaven (we can only speak in symbols) and cut
in half our minus sign—and make it a plus. Here is the centre
of salvation. When each of us admits himself a minus sign,
when in the just opinion of our friends—make no mistake—
we are all more or less minus signs, God comes on the scene
and says to each of us " so far as I am concerned you are creditable ! " " God commends His love to us in that while we
were yet sinners Christ died for us." Christ who knew no
sin, " became sin on our behalf that we might be creditable
to God through Christ." It is when a man grasps that this
is about him, and not just about other people in the same pew :
that so far as God is concerned " though his sins be as scarlet
they are now whiter than snow " ; then it is that he becomes
" a new creature " : he recovers his true nature as a co-operator
with God and not as the crucifier he has never wanted to be,

but has always degenerated to being! It is when he grasps this that he is back in the garden and *everything* in the garden is lovely. But it is inconceivable that this is, in any ordinary meaning of the word, an individual experience or a static experience. Cries St. Paul in the same chapter, " If any man be in Christ, he is a new creature: old things are passed away: behold, all things are become new." His environment changes with him. Nor can we rest in this experience, be static in it, for a solitary moment. The comfort resides in the ongoing experience of being Christ's hands and Christ's feet in the recovered co-operation now made possible. Thus the apostle, almost without a comma, inevitably goes on—" having committed to us the ministry of reconciliation."

" God was in Christ, reconciling the world to Himself, not counting against them their trespasses, and having committed to us the word of reconciliation." That is, if the Cross is first a catharsis, and then an inexpressible comfort, it must have a " contemporaneous," ongoing, consequence.

We are to be to others what Christ has become for us. The condition of our continuing conciliation with Him, is that we embark on the same unconditional reconciliation to others as He has extended to us. Someone has pointed out the psychological difference between a cross and a circle. A circle creates the impression of our being enclosed: say, in some field with a high wall and no gate. But a cross is that symbol opposed. Pointing infinitely upward and down, infinitely to right and left it spells unconditioned and unconditional freedom. It would be G. K. Chesterton who said that all religions are either " noughts or crosses." And if Christ came down so far to us so low, there can be but one consequence: our equally unconditioned desire to be forgiving to right hand and to left. Unless we are so engaged we are not saved: we have arrested the development of the work of the Cross. It becomes of "none" effect. "Forgive us our debts," runs strictly the Lord's Prayer, " as *we have forgiven* our debtors." Unless we are active on the horizontal level—that is unless we are involved with our neighbour domestically and politically, and indeed involved at the most difficult point of forgiveness— then we just cannot lay hold on our own forgiveness. We have arrested the development of the Cross and we are out of the garden and back in the desert with Cain and Abel, mouthing our brotherhood yet seeing our neighbour die; perhaps in Shanghai. Jesus tells of a certain king who forgave his servant a debt of about a million pounds. The servant thereupon went off to collect his own debt from a neighbour of about three pounds ten shillings. When the neighbour begged time, the forgiven servant cast him into prison till he should pay up. Forgiven from above he nonetheless exacted his due from his neighbour. Now Jesus does not say of that man that he was stingy or parsimonious or unimaginative or " a beginner in the Faith, who had the essential thing in him " : knowledge of his forgiveness. Jesus says of him that he was delivered by his Lord to the tormenters, *till he should pay all that was due.* And Jesus added, " So shall also my heavenly Father do unto you, if ye forgive not every one his brother from his heart." " If we forgive not men their trespasses, neither will our Father in heaven forgive us our trespasses." If we are not active on the horizontal level towards our neighbours, there is an arrestment in the work of the Cross.

We are not true to our nature in Christ. We are out of the garden and into the prison, until we are active again in the " love wherewith He loved us." Thus and thus it is in the Gospel: this inherence of social concern not just as a consequence of being saved, but as the very fibre of our being in a state of salvation.

The Church has always retained it in its intention. In the bidding prayer to the Communion in the Church of England it runs " Ye that do truly and earnestly repent you of your sins, and *are* in love and charity with your neighbours and intend to lead a new life . . . draw near . . . " But, though retained in our intention, do we carry the vertical and the horizontal as conjoined in our practice ?

If we did there would surely be a little less confusion about what is meant by " preaching the Gospel first " : a little less of the dismality whereby we prate " Trade Unionists are merely socially conscious, moving in one dimension, while we are two dimensional, seeing all things in the light of God " . . . only to find when we undertake a " war on want " that it is the merely one-dimensional who are prepared to give up a Saturday afternoon while the two-dimensional are almost entirely absent! The tragedy is that, by and large, the Trade Unionists **are** one-dimensional, caught in the thorn bush with Cain, prattling brotherhood and plotting privilege, while the saved, by and large, are absent either from the Trade Union or from the war on want!

IN SUMMARY

What has recognisably happened, if the crudity can be forgiven, is that we have dismembered the Cross. Churchmen carry about the vertical beam, our forgiveness in Christ, and unconsciously escape the turgid demands of its corollary in horizontal obedience. (Or do we do it consciously when we glimpse the measure of the cost?) While the world (oh so moral and well meaning!) carries round the horizontal, forever seeking right relations with neighbour man or neighbour nation, trying to get itself straight without that Bible knowledge about man's condition that humbles, and about the Christ that alone can totally exalt. Because it is not " engaged " the Faith becomes vacuous. Because it is blind, the world can never glimpse the only way to peace. It is precisely the conjunction of the vertical and the horizontal, that, in every sense, makes the Cross. And it is the Cross that alone can save.

*   *   *   *

Two short additional notes seem necessary. In the application of all this to the contemporary situation I am not a " perfectionist "—I am not arguing in effect that " if only Christians would become involved then we could expect the dawning of a new world of plenty, brotherhood and peace ! '' But I would share the strong conviction that if Christians do not more liberally add their salt to the boiling mixture that is the present turmoil then, bereft of seasoning, it will boil over to the scalding, it may be, of the whole world. This involvement is the King's business and it requireth haste.

Secondly, I have cast my case in political idiom because it is the nerve that most quickly awakes the passions of modern men. But, again, I am not pleading political concern to the exclusion of the multifarious interests and obligations of men. I am not really arguing that the mother of five children should leave them with a neighbour to address envelopes at Labour Headquarters, or that the doctor should scamp his patients' list to attend the Conservative Convention, or that the artist should leave his studio to paint posters for the Economic League. I simply argue that the Cross be raised again at the centre of the market-place as well as on the steeple of the church. I am recovering the claim that Jesus was not crucified in a cathedral between two candles, but on a cross between two thieves ; on the town garbage-heap ; at a crossroad so cosmopolitan that they had to write his title in Hebrew and in Latin and in Greek (or shall we say in English, in Bantu and in Afrikaans ?) ; at the kind of place where cynics talk smut, and thieves curse, and soldiers gamble. Because that is where He died. And that is what He died about. And that is where churchmen should be and what churchmanship should be about.

SHOULD THE CHURCH CONFINE ITSELF TO THE GOSPEL ?

This was the question that we posed. The answer is '' Yes '' ; provided we realise that the Gospel has no confines.

'' Let us leave behind the elementary teaching about Christ and go forward to adult understanding. Let us not lay over and over again the foundation truths. No, if God allows, let us go on.''

The one remaining way for churchmen, the one way left, is to recover the full proportions of the Faith.

CHAPTER THREE

THE DARKNESS OF MISSION

Invited to give a course of lectures, it is good to ask why? Not because of any theological insights granted me, would my name be considered. Perhaps it was because no man can spend twenty years in parish mission, his own and others, and in the furtherance of youth work, without amassing perhaps six hints that might be exalted into six lectures.

Now, had the Trustees of this Lectureship—in an even greater departure from wisdom—chosen me three years earlier, I would have elaborated such hints with a certain show of confidence even though they might have been received "without benefit to clergy."

My predicament is this. In the last three years I have come to a conclusion that has almost unseated me from the charger on which I rode. I am now convinced that no mission will match our day that is not infused with a quite revolutionary recovery of certain theological insights. I am not unlike the unhappy mediaeval knight in a castle in Asia Minor. Like many other knights, as they approached the actual encounter of the great crusade, he was suffering from cold feet, physical and emotional. Peter the Hermit, summoned to re-enthuse them, was so successful that with one accord all the other knights had leapt to their feet, tumultuously shouting "to the Holy Land!" Even now they were all cavorting into the castle-yard demanding of the varlets that the horses at once be saddled. In the hall of the great oration only Peter was left with our unhappy knight sitting disconsolate, biting his nails amidst a sea of discarded agenda papers creaming round his bench. Said Peter, noticeably peeved that his peroration had not had unanimous response, "But are you not going too?" "I don't know," mumbled the frustrated knight. "And why?" asked Peter. "Because," said the knight, "I've been there."

Well, for twenty years, I have been there : in parish mission and in Christian social action with youth groups . . . and . . . " I don't know." Short of a recovery of certain theological insights, I just don't believe we will recover the beleaguered city, and make comely in the sight of men the Holy Vistas. As in Kipling's poem *The Explorer*, there is " Something lost behind the ranges." Hence my embarrassment. It means my projecting some theological insights ; I who am not a theologian.

Two thoughts alone prevent complete confusion of face. Firstly, my insights have come not as they come, and no doubt ought to come, to trained theologians in the thrust and parry of intellectual debate ; but in the heat and confusion of constant parley with men and women of every station who manifestly need God. They are men and women, moreover, who in large measure want us to show Him to them and who yet turn away, not contemptuously, to other gods, but sadly : because our engagement with them has not, in experience, exposed them to the nature of their sickness, far less introduced them to Him who alone can heal. I come, that is, from the battlefield, in disjointed phrases to report. I come in what I believe is a dark hour of mission : seeing the issues no more clearly than as trees walking. This is not an unusual way to see things in raids before dawn. I come in the hope that, in the lighted apartments of calm headquarters, those better equipped may grasp the lasting import of these splutterings and give them due proportion in their larger strategy.

A second thought encourages. " The Word of God " is not a written statement but a living Person. The Bible is but the cradle for the Saviour-Child. Victory, spiritual or military, has never ensued from a correct order of battle : far less from a correct statement of the Cause. The intention and the action are indissolubly twined.

Such introduction may enlighten the pattern I have chosen. Firstly, the crisis of mission. The next chapter would identify the issues that I see as trees walking, which may begin to point the way out. In the next three chapters we dare St. Paul's own method of approach: opening with the principles of recovered mission and then not scorning, in each, such pedestrian conclusions as may implement these principles in practice. Thus we will review the principle and practice in the work of the congregation; in the worship of the congregation: and in the relationship of the congregation to the world outside. For society, equally with the congregation, is under the kingship of Christ: " God sent not His Son to condemn the world but that the *world* through Him might be saved." The final chapter will deal with the devotional life of the church-member in this setting, if all our best laid schemes are not to go agley.

THE CRISIS OF MISSION TO-DAY

What is Mission ? At an army boxing tournament in France, between two bouts, they led round the ring a soldier from hospital who had lost his memory. The hope was that from the army corps of spectators with whom he had served one man at least might recognise him, and so assist his cure. None however did. As the man, frustrated, was led down from the ring he threw out his arms and cried, " Will nobody tell me who I am ? " Such is the cry of increasing multitudes to-day. The task of Christian mission is no more or less than to tell man who he is; with all that results from his hearing. The crisis of mission is to tell him that he " hears."

But the darkness of our present plight can also be projected in a story. An Oxford scholar, and convinced Christian, with a brilliant career half-completed in the Colonial Service, threw it up to run a boys' club in London. Appalled by the complete aimlessness of even his most senior and responsible lads, he embarked on a course of twenty instructions on succeeding Sunday nights. He gave the Christian answer to " Who am I ? " over against all the other answers, spoken and unspoken, that mould the conduct of youth in a modern city. Rest assured he knew the answer, spoke in their own language and obeyed all the laws of " communication." Thirty young men embarked on the course. At the end there were only seven. Finally he asked Bill, the ablest of the stickers, " Have I proved my case ? " " Yes, sir," said Bill, " you have proved it up to the hilt : *and it doesn't mean a thing.*"

The disembodied Word is not enough. Even correctly stated it is not the Word at all. But such is so obvious a cliché, that we might pause a minute. Before probing the darkness we might go into a parenthesis, albeit " in block capitals." For this parenthesis contains a conviction, clearer than a tree walking, which I carry from the battlefield. Indeed it is the conviction that will be the recurring theme of these chapters. Its essence is this : we have largely dropped from our declaration of the Gospel the one aspect that makes our Faith unique. Put it this way :—

" Yes sir," said Bill, " you have proved your case up to the hilt ; and it doesn't mean a thing." As these words are addressed mainly to budding clergy, I suggest that at that terrifying moment the correct reply, in terms of typical theological discussion—and however incomprehensible to Bill— would be, " Young man, you have out-Bultmanned Bultmann."

Bultmann is a theologian. And the general reader probably assumes at this point that he will now have to skip, or even give up reading this book, so convinced is he that we are now moving into the realm of the unintelligible. But theologians deal with quite living issues ! Even the man in the pew, these last twenty years, must have been conscious of two types among the preachers whom he has heard. Roughly the preachers of to-day are either " orthodox " or " liberal " : that is either they preach the Word, full of texts, with a rather vague application, or they deal with particular modern instances, rather vaguely relating them to a Bible text " here and there." The man in the pew is a little perplexed ! He feels the man with the texts is obviously more " religious " but usually unintelligible : while the man with the modern instances is very interesting but doubtfully " religious " ! The name of Karl Barth is usually associated with the " orthodox " recovery, while most ministers over forty-five years of age are " liberal."

Now the significance of Rudolph Bultmann is that he is neither. And a leading British thinker describes his work as a " major turning point in the history of the impact of Christian thought on the world." Both Barth and Bultmann put to the preacher the same question, " Are you giving to your hearers the Word of God or a set of human ideas ? " But, whereas Barth is asking whether modern ideas are being substituted for God's message, Bultmann is afraid we preachers are so conversant with the thought forms current two thousand years ago that our very way of thinking, and therefore speaking, comes between our hearers and the word of God. While Barth would recall us to a stern message, whether men " understood " it or not, Bultmann would claim that preachers must start where men are and not where the preacher would like them to be! Thus for Bultmann, the preacher has not only the duty of truth, of presenting the Message as it has been given him, but also of love, so presenting his message that men *can* hear it, so that, if they do not, the fault is in them and not in the preacher. What he urges is that so long as we insist on presenting men with Christ *plus* the world view of the first century then certain " thought forms " like the Creation story, the Resurrection, the Ascension, the " return " of Christ are so unintelligible to modern man, so *myth*-ical, that modern man sleeps through them and escapes the offence of the Cross. Thus, he says, we must *de*-mythologise the Bible, in order to confront modern man with the living Christ.*

With humility, I do not think Bultmann has hit the real crisis. Bill, I claim, presented the deeper problem when he said to his club leader, " You have proved it up to the hilt and it doesn't mean a thing! " For Bill, representative of modern man, is not confused by the myth, else he would not have felt the case proved. I claim it is not the mythical form

---

*For this inadequate description of Bultmann's position I am indebted to a larger analysis by Rev. E. L. Allen, Ph.D., D.D., in the *Preachers Quarterly* for June, 1955.

that makes man deaf. *It is the vacuity we have created at the centre of the myth.* For consider:

God surely knew what He was doing when He gave all Holy Scriptures to be written for men's learning in all generations; knew that in every century all children love a story and, at a very early age, can grasp that all worthwhile stories have inner meanings. They know that only some literalist folly would attempt to unravel the exact relation between the inner meaning and the outward form. It is, for instance, surely a sorry cove who would trouble to unravel the story of Jack and the Beanstalk: leaving Jack and his beanstalk as the constant element and cutting out the castle at the top as uncongenial to the limitations of a television screen. And if some theologian here protests that demythologising is not a system of subtraction but the creation of modern formulas of communication, then we must wait on Bultmann's attempt to convey " the new look " that would be given to, say, the opening of Genesis, before deciding whether confusion would not be worse confounded.

Man's faculty to see through the myth to its abiding truth is within the capacity of every age: whether in the angelic and demonic world of the Bible, or the folklore of the mediaevalists, or indeed in the " myth " offered by the physicists— that the ultimate nature of the atom is " light/energy." Relative pictures alone can convey the ultimate.

No. If we are to set the eyes of men " beyond history " again, get them convinced there is more to living than life with a small " l," we must see the issue as " behind Bultmann." *What we must do for Bill, and modern man, is not to demythologise the Bible but to rehumanise the area and content of our Salvation.* With or without benefit of " liberals," we must recover the shattering claim of the writer of the Epistle to the Hebrews that there is a Man in Heaven: and that this Man came down: and that this Man reigns: and that it is this Man who will come at the last, in like manner as they saw Him going, to judge the earth.

44

It is quite true that in the early part of our century, such was the optimism of western man about progress till " 1914-18," and such the pathological desire for a warless world after that holocaust, that the pulpit gave to men a series of humanistic hopes only vaguely related to the clear Biblical dictates of the Word of God. It was to be expected, and salutary, that a protest should come, such as one associates with Karl Barth. But dare we claim that one does not correct too humanistic views of the possibility of man, by leaving intact equally unscriptural visions of the nature of the Divine Majesty ? If Jesus is like God, then God is like Jesus : loving, suffering, triumphant. It is this that was a " stumbling-block to the Jews and sheer folly to the Greeks." But it is this that is the power and wisdom of God to them that believe. It is this that is forever a stumbling-block to the moral element in each of us and folly to the philosophic element in each of us : that the everlasting God and King is forever like the Man Jesus !

It is not that His almightiness is any less absolute than that of the most absolute Eastern potentate. He is absolute power but that power resides in His love. " We do not see all things subject unto Him; but we do see *Jesus* crowned with glory and with honour." This is the shocking uniqueness of the Christian Faith—that a Man reigns in Heaven : and that this Man will come again.

This is the Myth way, the true " story way," of declaring that the determinative fact about the " end," and therefore the determinative fact about all we do now towards that end, is that it is about the possibilities of Man. Thus, with or without benefit of " liberals," our task is to recover, for instance, in our thinking and acting, the shattering offer of the Book of the Revelation that the end is not catastrophe but consummation. For that book comes to its climax not in the destruction of all things but in the restoration of all things. It is about the Heavenly Jerusalem coming down. The end is not an atomic explosion followed by thin air, but a crisis whose fulfilment will be a city with streets, a community in perfect response to a Man glorified, in Whose hands are still the marks of the nails and in Whose side is still the scar of a sword-thrust. How much more substantial is this hope than the individualist offer of immortality to which our Faith has degenerated : as if the end were not this glorious consummation but some catastrophe in which a select few, apparently, will be shot " up " to enjoy a perpetual concert. (For, whether we like it or not, it is something like that which modern man rejects when he fails to be concerned with our offers of immortality. And how Biblically right he is.)

Bultmann started on his quest (and bless him for every risk he takes) because the German soldiers passed by the offer of the Message. But what made them, and modern man, pass by is not the obstacle of mythological concepts : *but our dehumanising of Him who is our sole Salvation.* The tragic turning aside of German soldiers to the delirium tremens of Hitler's myth of " blood and soil " was manifestly not because they could not be moved by a myth. They died by the million for a myth ! It was because we would not let them drink from the rock that was Christ. It is because we have made a haloed myth of Christ Himself, and not a Rock, that the passions of men become demonic. The passions of men are built for nothing less than intoxication—" that divine intoxication more sober than sobriety itself," as an early Father described the Faith. It is the intoxication of love. And the Rock which followed God's people in the wilderness was to sustain " the people Israel," the community of His love. Nor will men find Him, as one to satisfy our age, till we recover again His most glorious humanity in which that community is already set. It is that which we have mythologised. We have subtracted the Man Jesus from the Godhead leaving an Eastern potentate in control and a pale Galilean suffering off stage. Till we are baptised again into His humanity as it is now enthroned in the everlasting Godhead, the myth will not mean a thing. The human Jesus that the liberals recovered must be enthroned again at the heart of the Father Almighty to Whom the orthodox recalled us.

Then let the Bible view have full course again. But how straitened will we be, by any such Baptism, till it be accomplished.

Such then is our " block capital " parenthesis, raising many a " but " and " if you mean " for the reader. Yet it is the burden of this book to expand it.

With this pointer to the area in which we are working, let us return to what is meant by the darkness of mission. Let us dare a picture of where we have got to in history to-day. We have come to a point, I would claim, so climactic that it might be called a new epoch in history.

DO WE GRASP THE DIMENSION OF OUR TIME ?

In Germany three years ago I spoke to a group of Germans on the fall of Adam. At question-time a young German girl asked, " Do you think the atom is the second apple ? " What did she mean ? Are we, she might have asked, on the edge of an age almost as revolutionary as that point when Man was given individual choice ? Here I ask patience for a simile whose purpose is to picture the plight of modern man. We have written of him as isolated, increasingly asking what is his significance. Thus I want to draw a parallel between him and John the Baptist.

A SIMILE

John Baptist came at the end of a dispensation. Can we see him in that significance and then draw a parallel to modern man ?

Whatever more fundamental lesson we may draw from the Garden of Eden, at least it marked a new development in the relation of God to man. When man said " No " to God, he started on his long road to independence. God's own purpose for man almost necessitated that divorce, so that man might be free at the last to find for himself his dependence. And then find his interdependence with men through Christ. Like the prodigal son, man had to go into a far country and find

47

dereliction before he could know for himself how living and free is the love of the Father.

But the Eden story was only a symbol independence. Man, so to say, only started on his independence. Despite the initial thrust, man remained, for untold centuries, a tribal being: part of a collective whole. Methuselah, for instance, in his apparent great age, really covers the history of several generations who felt themselves part and parcel of one life, as an African tribe feels to-day. Again when Abraham received a promise " for his seed " it was not felt as a promise to Abraham, his son and grandson. The promise was felt as a totality to " Abraham-and-his-seed." The people Israel, starting from Ur of the Chaldees, took into their tribal consciousness the whole Chaldean wisdom. It was still a totality that moved into Egypt and imbibed Egyptian wisdom: that moved into the Promised Land, were driven into exile, and returned to Jerusalem as a people. Tribe: corpus: God's collective—such is the essential instrument through which God dealt under the old Covenant, till the group task was over and the community dispersed. The Maccabees, if you like, were the final flare-up of the old collectivism: the Resistance Movement that failed. Then the light went out.

To be sure, this collective consciousness was not uniformly sustained. In and through the collective consciousness of relationship to God, the individual was gradually shaking out. For instance, the size of the group dwindles; Shem thought the promise was to a race: Abraham thought it was to a nation: finally it was to the tribe of a nation. Again when we read that Noah and his sons got drunk: it is not really a sad episode in the history of morals. They were followers of a mystic cult: using a serious technique to be dissociate from group consciousness. Noah's initiation experiments with wine were a thrust towards individualism. This shaking out is there too in the vision of Ezekiel—" the *soul* that sinneth it shall die " : a vision terrific for its time.

Such, in brief, is the relationship of person to community

48

in the Old Testament. The group as God's instrument; the group becoming less significant; the clan disintegrating; the individual breaking loose.

It is in some such process that I ask you to see John Baptist. " A voice crying in the wilderness " can be translated " a voice crying in absolute solitude." It is not just that he so cried : it is that in the person of John there is the end of the long process. He is the last and he is alone : a voice crying in absolute solitude. What insight against that dereliction to cry " Prepare " ! Yes, indeed, " of men born of women none was greater than John." Yet such was the isolation that Jesus had also to say, " He that is least in the Kingdom is greater than he."

So it was then, just then (the awful loneliness of the human race typified in the last of the true Israel), " *when the fulness of time was come*, God sent His Son, born of a woman, born under the Law." Into that moment of history Christ came : the new Man and the new start. Christ the new Man who, in His own person, was also *the new community*. We must not forget that Jesus carried most mysteriously in His own person the whole history of Israel. Jesus who was recognised by the wise men of Chaldea, whence Abraham had come : who in His infancy went down into Egypt where Israel had been : who went into the wilderness for forty days, as Israel had gone : who finally was Himself the Passover, carries " all Israel " into the Holy of Holies to open the kingdom of heaven to all believers. Jesus the new person, was also the new community, the new family, *world-wide and moral, not just tribal and instinctive.*

ITS APPLICATION

Now is there not in this a parallel to our modern plight and the introduction to the answer ? Is there not here a clue to the isolation of modern man and the beginning of the answer for him in Christ ? Dare we compare modern man to this significance of John ?

Part of our sickness is that Christianity has become an

individual affair. But has that been long in the consciousness of man ?

What did the individual soul, for instance, know of salvation when Constantine, in the fourth century, first made Christianity the authorised religion of the Roman Empire ? It is well not to forget how Europe was christianised. It might almost be said that in the *Daily Roman Express* one Saturday one might have seen in a small paragraph on the back page, a passing reference to the persecution of some Christians, who were still a forbidden sect. But in the Monday edition there were banner headlines on the front page, " You Are All Christians Now." A rude fellow has described that tremendous act in history as " Baptism by hosepipe." Did the individual enter an experience ? Again through the Middle Ages, it was surely by a group faith that the vast majority were kept spiritually alive. Again we pretend the Reformation was an individual choice : but for the majority of folk was Calvin's restored theocracy different in common experience from their membership together in " Rome " ? Certainly, as in our parallel, through all these centuries the individual was emerging, with an instance here and there, till at the Reformation there was a bubbling up of personal consciousness as the Holy Empire broke up into nationalisms, and the consciousness of villages into the consciousness of families. John Bunyan, with his new conception of the whole burden on one man's back ; William Law, with his call to personal holiness are typical exceptions, prophets of the coming individualist flood. But for the generality, whether it was the cottar on a Saturday night, or the Covenanters at Drumclog, how corporate, tribal, instinctive, was the Faith of Scotland. Till, again as in our parallel, it all winnows down to the stark individualism of the 19th century when finally the corpus, national and ecclesiastical, broke down. The Evangelicals, perhaps, were the Maccabees making a last desperate attempt to keep the sense of a corpus in Christ. But even the 19th century revivals degenerated into the individualism that was their environment.

Till the time of living memory, our religion was essentially tribal. The mass of men in their faith were like leaves organically adhering to a living tree, part of a corporate growth. But the last century was the autumn. Men became dessicated, forced to discover an individualist Faith, the real corpus having dried up.

Now, in the twentieth century, it is winter and we cannot get growth again. Nor can there be a new spring except in Christ. Men must have community. The appeal of Hitler was that he knew this. He said to Germany, " I will make you feel together again ": and they fell for him almost to a man: for he dealt with western man at his driest and most consciously individual. They were like dessicated leaves. What desperate experience it was for defeated Germany to discover that all that Hitler had done was to sweep them into a bucket—to make them feel together again. Of Grace, our own land was saved that tragedy but we are not much better than dried and dessicated leaves.

It is still winter and we cannot get growth again. We have our Bible weeks. Why are not folk reading the Bible ? Because of science ? No. Because they cannot find comfort in it for individualist salvation ; for the Bible is about salvation for persons in community.

In Church organisation we struggle and strive to build community again by a host of new techniques—oh, the noble pathos of our activism ! We strive to make our congregations cohere, that life may seem coherent, but they fall apart, in the summer, until laboriously we gear in again to another shot at winter activities, with new hints, new drives, new tricks. A seven years stretch of it, in one parish, is sufficient to drain the strength of a modern minister. The finer the intent the greater is the drain. It is because we dare not look at the real condition of modern man.

He is a voice crying in absolute solitude. And he is this at a moment when, as never before, he has the means to control his environment. " At last," wrote Chesterton, " one man can sit at a microphone and address the entire world: now that man has nothing to say."

OUR HOPE

However, " He that is down need fear no fall." " In the fullness of time God sent His Son . . . " In the measure that we are at the end of an old dispensation, in that measure we are come to a new fullness of the time. God who designed dependence so that in the first stage of His revelation men might know His providence : Who then allowed Independence that men might know their need, now calls us to Interdependence. An old voice speaks again, " Prepare ye this way for the Lord."

As God, in His vast design, rolled up tribal community till John Baptist stood alone, so He has rolled up our tribal, instinctive Christian communities. It is God who has also rolled up even the appearance of satisfaction in individualistic Christianity. It is God who has rolled up Christendom. Christendom has had a great fall, and not all the Vatican horses nor all the ecumenical men will ever put Christendom together again, in any authoritarian way.

God has rolled up instinctive Christendom because He wants it built of really free persons at last, and for the first time, voluntarily choosing Him and His way, but choosing Him as the new community. He has rolled up even the possibility of individual religion by itself alone, till we learn that we cannot become persons except in community. Not until we pay as much attention to Christian community as to personal conversion, to God's pattern for our world—if you like, to God's " politic " —can we know the meaning of persons again or dare to talk of personal conversion, though its spurious counterfeit may continue to deceive.

Some reader may here be protesting, " All the writer is after is that we must see God as a God of history ! " and may be adding to himself, " but that has been on every Christian teacher's lips for two decades." Yes : on their lips, but in our lives ? What means a recovery of a belief in God as a God of history ? Well, what of Africa from Cape Town, via Kenya, to Morocco ? In what theological college are they adequately discussed ? In what theological college is it even apparent that they ought to be discussed; except perhaps in the passage as men go out to luncheon. Is it at such a periphery that we adequately come to terms with God's community as He moves in history ?

Again a reader may interject, " the writer merely pleads a recovery of the Doctrine of the Church: surely in every theological hall such is now in the centre of discussion, and in many congregations—where the congregation is now called ' the instrument of mission '." Well, these chapters are couched in terms of the congregation but it is no good lisping a doctrine of the Church as if it were a slightly tarnished doctrine that requires a little rubbing up.

It is because we put the vast problems of " God's community " second—and a long way second—that increasingly folk are asking, " Will nobody tell me who I am ? " And when we answer in merely theoretic terms, " it does not mean a thing." It is no good saying with a passionate gleam in the eye, " there is one solution for Africa—One Faith, One Lord, One Baptism," and then moving at a snail's pace about Church Unity there, where there are 269 registered Christian denominations. *There* is a problem of God's community. It is no good saying of Kenya, " What is wanted there is a Christian conviction such as only the West can give " : and then going at a snail's pace about the fact that the average European income there is some £600 a year; and the average income of such Africans as are industrial workers is less than £50 a year. *There* is a problem of God's community. It is because we put the problems of God's community second that increasingly folk will continue to be restless. Restless till they rest in Him. And to rest in God is not to ascend to some high spiritual mysticism. To rest in God is to be lost in community that *we* may be found in Him. A fullness of the time has come when obedience to Christ as the new community is the only way to be comforted of Him as the new Man.

How is it that we fail to declare it ? Not for want of trying I admit. I claim this community will not be recovered by the congregation, and therefore not proffered to the world for its acceptance or rejection, till we re-humanise the Message: recover for men the Vision of a Man in Heaven and fall down with them in awe at the knowledge that the apex of His majesty resides in His most glorious humanity.

To close, let us go back to the " front line " where I learnt these things. Another reader may be saying, " But all this is just sociology with religious nobs on." There is the crux. For is not the evolving story of the Bible from Genesis to the Revelation what we would now call a sociology ? It is our forgetfulness of this that has allowed us to mythologise the Christian offer of Salvation.

When I was in South Africa, just prior to a big public meeting in Durban an unknown Ulsterman approached me and said, " I hope you are going to give them the Gospel red hot." " Yes," I replied, " I am speaking of its social implications here in Durban." " Social implications ? " he repeated in an acme of suspicion, " What is wanted is the Gospel red hot." " But is it not of the Gospel," I asked, " that by right of Christ all men have an equal dignity ? " " Yes," he said, " that is of the Gospel." " Then what," I said, " are you Gospellers doing about the ten thousand Africans and Indians who have not got a decent shelter in Durban this cold night ? " " Them ? " replied the hot Gospeller, " I wish the whole damn lot were sunk in the harbour ! " Yet that man could have recited the whole Christian offer immaculately, and his own engagement to be in Christ.

What had happened ? We had allowed him to mythologise the Gospel offer itself. He had never really faced the terrible challenge that the apex of the divine majesty resides for ever in Christ's most glorious humanity.

But perhaps you would fob me off with " that is just some

fundamental pietist who has lost the way." " Scotland," you would say, " is embarking on a rounded mission of the Church, with the Church as the community in the forefront." But be careful that we do not still embrace the darkness. For consider this. Go, indeed more responsibly, to the finest extant expression of what Calvinism has become in our world to-day: to the Dutch Reformed Church in South Africa. I take it, if we visualise a Church revival in our land, the sort of marks we would expect would be . . . a Church among whose membership the Bible was daily open—family prayers the rule: a Church instructed with full doctrinal sermons, and not just sermonettes with some such title as *Paddles round Patmos with Paul*. A Church with great sacramental occasions, with due preparation and restored Mondays of Thanksgiving. A Church of generous giving, because they know the richness of the Gospel to be shared. A Church of missionary enthusiasm, because all should hear the releasing Word. But all that is precisely a description of the Dutch Reformed Church! Their missionary offers of service exceed all the other denominations combined. Their achieved budgets per head absolutely beggar our standards. Their sacramental occasions and devotional obedience put ours to shame and . . . *they are directly responsible for the most reactionary social insights in all Western Christendom.* They are piling high their utterly sincere devotions on the altar of a myth, because they have mythologised the pivot point of the Gospel of Christ. They have failed to grasp that the apex of the heavenly majesty is His eternal and most glorious humanity. No doubt you here say, " But surely our own land is not either pietist in its indifference, like that misled Ulsterman, not blind in its social constructions, as the deviating Dutch Reformed. We have had a commission on Communism, with a full-time organiser, so conscious are we of its importance. We publish their reports that all the laity may read. We have enjoined special classes for elders that in industrial places lay leaders may be informed. We have our social action groups among youth. We have integrated The Iona Community to focus our obligations to get into politics, industry and the rest." In a word, you ask, are we not humanised enough? But what really is the response? When the General Assembly discussed the Communism Report, how many of the 1,500 commissioners attended? Around two hundred. How many of its reports were purchased, when *Life and Work* has a circulation of a quarter of a million? Around three thousand. When Community House in Glasgow approached thirty enthusiastic ministers in industrial areas, asking that each personally contact three elders or leading laymen to attend a ten weeks' class in the simplest outline of the issues between Christianity and Communism, so that a maximum ninety might get back to their place of work and know just a few of the answers, how many laymen turned up to the class? Precisely none. Or, to be fair, one man came, who had not been invited, as he was thinking of becoming a Communist but wanted to know what Christianity was about.

What is the interpretation, of Ulsterman, of Dutch Reformed, of our own witness, in their varying backgrounds? Surely it is not spiritual defection in its ordinary sense, nor gross blindness of heart. Charlatanry is absent. Is it not the deeply-rooted conviction that all such issues are the periphery of our work, a distant derivative of our Faith whose main engagement lies elsewhere? Is it not a continuing conviction that the Message stands consistent within itself: and that the Church can become revitalised within the borders of its own domain: from which domain, at some date always projected into the future, it will seriously close with the claims of Christ in society?

But our God is a God that moves. If we seek to confine Him to Church circles, "He abideth faithful. But He cannot deny His own nature." He remains Sovereign of all. Inexorably His laws work out.

For fifty years God has played His music to us through the events of history to win us again to the challenge of community. At the turn of the century, in the Boer war, we heard the opening chords of His Song of Judgment, if we continued longer with our independent Empires. In 1914-18 there began a fuller orchestration of His warning. In 1939-45, every instrument was brought to bear in a crescendo of appeal. At its close He spoke to us in the shattering piercing whistle of the first atom bomb.

" I have authorised its use," said the First Citizen of the World, " that nations may be forced to find other means of settling international disputes." To-day ? We have invented a bomb two thousand five hundred times as potent and we manufacture them in hundreds. " Tell me," said the German girl, " do you think the atom is the second apple ? "

Will you not agree there is a terrifying darkness about our Mission ? Till we pierce it, our clarion calls to the outsider hardly mean a thing.

CHAPTER FOUR

A PRINCIPLE OF RECOVERY

This chapter, at the centre of our book, is a uniting bridge. The chapters that follow will be concerned with how a more adequate sense of community can be recovered in the life and worship of our congregations. But there is a principle of God's methods with His people which must again be enthroned in our consciousness if these activities are to bear fruit.

We have surveyed the crisis of mission: man not knowing who he is: and further not being able to " hear " because of the collapse of the community in which he used to be set. We have admitted the awareness of the Church of this collapse and the plethora of its efforts to correct it. But we have had to note its failure adequately to make the grade. Exploring this failure, we have argued, in a parenthesis and a conclusion, that our fundamental dis-ease lies in our mythologising of " Him with whom we have to do." We have forgotten the central uniqueness of our Faith: that the apex of the divine majesty resides in Christ's most glorious humanity. We have overlaid the significance of the claim that there is a Man in Heaven and that He who so ascended shall come in like manner to judge the earth.

But there is a conjoined recovery that we must make. In a sentence it is this: *only in a living total fellowship can this Word of God be correctly heard.* This is the method God Himself has ordained.

A FORMAL APPROACH

Let us put it this way. The formal introduction to recovery would be an excursion into theology. Such excursion might be a discourse on modern trends in " dogmatic " theology. On paper they appear very fruitful for our purpose. In the doctrine of the *Trinity*, some responsible thinkers now call for the substitution of the old metaphysical relationship between the three persons in the Trinity. The older description almost conveyed the picture of Three Persons fulfilling their complementary functions in rotation. These moderns would substitute rather what one of them has called the " communityness " of the Three Persons. Consequent on such a way of stating it, we could well argue that our social obligations rest not just on ethical grounds (the duty to love our neighbour) but inhere in the very nature of the Godhead in eternity. Thus social involvement is not a matter of ethical obedience but a condition of being in communion with God at all.

Or again—and cognate of course—the creation of a community on earth not just as a long term policy for the few, but as an immediate obligation on all, arises from the recovered Augustinian doctrine of the *Holy Spirit*. The thought of St. Augustine here is that the Holy Spirit is the love wherewith the Father loves the Son and the Son loves the Father. Thus the Holy Spirit is the lively link binding the Father and the Son together. In virtue of what He is, the Holy Spirit is the ground and the bond of our Fellowship together on earth. Consequent on such recovery our whole obligation of earthly fellowship becomes revolutionised in its immediacy. Again, this creation of community on earth, inherent in our response to the Trinity, is implied, if not explicit, in the " dimensional approach " as it could be figured from Martin Buber.

Or it could be argued from those who tell us how God reveals Himself. These protest that God is not directly discerned but mediated through another: that " the God revealed is the God concealed " and that only at the level of fellowship can we come to know Him.

Thus and thus, the formal introduction to recovery could be an excursion into modern theological trends : building up to a crescendo of demand that we must " find community," not as a derived duty but to be in communion with God at all.

BUT WHO IS IN FORM ?

Yet this is not our line : not only because I am not equipped, save for a tedious expansion of others' themes, but because I do not see these exciting restatements issuing forth in action in the lives of those most enthusiastic in their advocacy ! I do not see them involved at the horizontal level of social concern as one might assume from their descriptions of what is implied in communion with God. If these things happen in the green tree what will happen in the dry ? If the men with the new insights are listless, how gross is the darkness for the rest of us ?

If this way of stating it were gratuitously insulting, as I fear it must sound, I hope I would refrain from it. Insult is not my purpose. The listlessness is not of laziness. Dead intellectualism is no more my charge, than charlatanry was my charge against the Ulsterman with his mythologised conception of Salvation, or hypocrisy my charge against the Dutch Reformed, with their sincere ecclesiastical devotion. I put it thus because there is a deficiency of insight concerning how God works, which prevents us all from really hearing. Return to our last theological insight—that God is not directly discerned but mediated through other people ; and that it is only at the level of fellowship that we can come to know God. If this be true there is a sense in which we are all inhibited from true theological insight by our forgetfulness, in experience, of the kind of community in which God is interested. It follows that even a crescendo of correct statements only deafens the ears, unless the hearer is actually set in the kind of community in which God is interested.

THE WINCE

Somehow we must come at it the other way. We will get nowhere with statements, however correct, till we come level, in our own lives, with God's decision that *economic values are inherent in the community of His Love*. It is this sort of deficiency in our consciousness that withers away our revivals.

And the wince that you felt in—what Chaucer would have called—your guts when I stated it so bluntly is the proof of my pudding. And let me quickly add that the wince gets me just as much: and in the same place. We have in Scotland a long term National Home Mission project that we call " Tell Scotland." The slogan is based on our Lord's words sent to John Baptist in prison, " Tell John, that to the poor the Gospel is preached." Now if we spiritualise the Gospel to mean some spiritual unguent to thicken the skin against the arrows of economic uncertainty or injustice, you take your stand with our Ulsterman: the red hot Gospel is purely transcendental. But we have all discarded any such disembodied Faith. In our interlaced world we know the economic is the rub and squirm because we know it. When we read of troubles in Kenya and pray for our steadfast missions there that tolerance, through them, may somehow be recovered, it gets us some-where in the pit of our stomach when we read—as we did earlier—that 1 per cent of the population has an income of £650 a year and the average African wage earner (including emoluments) averages less than £50 a year. (Wage earners exclude those in the rural areas whose economic status cannot be computed in cash.) And when we realise further that the European 1 per cent are the Christians, we know that there is the rub. " Tell John, that to the poor the Gospel is preached." The economic is the rub, but so little is its inherence in the Gospel in our consciousness we think they must first get the dogma of the Trinity . . . and then, . . . perhaps, . . . later, . . . all that wincing stuff.

Or when we read that one hundred Priest Workers have been disbanded in France, by the Roman Hierarchy, because they have made the nearest modern shot at being identified with the poor (as surely Jesus was, with the same reaction from the traditionalists) in order to " preach the Gospel to the poor," and when we read that all the progressives in the Roman Church are shaken lest the proletariat be now swallowed back into Communism, we know the economic is the rub.

But so little is its inherence in the Gospel in our consciousness that we remain complacent for, after all, " is not the Church devising new descriptions for the work of the Holy Spirit which one day . . . etc."

Such and such declares the divergence between the Word and the kind of community in which God is interested.

We have not, please note, stated that God is primarily interested in economic community. Yet that these values are inherent in the community He would build can hardly be gainsaid by anyone who takes seriously Holy Writ.

What is therefore here purposed is an examination of the Hebrew revelation of how God acts with His people.

THE HEBRAIC VIEWPOINT

Let us attempt a few ejaculatory hints that may assist us to recover the Hebrew mind.

There is first their peculiar claim that the residence of the Spirit is in the blood. The " Kosher " meat of the orthodox Hebrew has the blood drained from it originally for this mystic reason. As the blood forever courses through the body, so for the Hebrew spiritual values were linked with what was occurring in the body politic—that is, in their ordinary ongoing history. And, just as if you separate blood from body the blood dries and the body dies, so if you separate spiritual concerns from social the former become vacuous and the latter crack up. It is our failure to think in these terms that makes us imagine, quite erroneously, that you can deal with the Gospel first and that the rest will follow. Secondly, to recover the Hebrew approach, we must remember their peculiar connotation of truth. For them truth was not so much a static noun as an active verb. Man's relation to God was not in response to a set of principles that could be exalted into a series of " truths " but was an active ongoing betrothal— literally a be-truth-al, best described as a " Covenant." Our failure so to think, again, causes us to attempt to convince men of certain Gospel truths in the hope that—sometime—

their application will follow. In fact, however, if it isn't an ongoing betrothal, a fatal divorce is established from the start. Thirdly, we must recover what holiness meant to the Hebrew. In the common speech of Queen Elizabeth's time, current when our Bible was translated, holiness had the connotation that we would now associate with healthiness. An Elizabethan group of peasants, seated on the village green and seeing a child skipping past, full of the joy of spring, would normally remark " what a holy child " : not thereby conveying she had just received a diploma at the Sunday school but that she was " all in " healthy. Thus when the reverend gentlemen sat round that table of Bible translation, poring over the Hebrew, the Latin and the Greek originals before them, and chose the word holy, what they had in mind was much nearer what we would now call healthiness than the thought conveyed to our modern minds by the word holy. And if the reader here exclaims " the author is disgracefully debasing the final word left us to denote God's absolute transcendence," I must be patient, for I agree that all is lost if we lose sight of holy as the description of God's absolute transcendence. But the reader must be patient also. For the whole " offence " of the Christian revelation is its claim that the apex of the divine majesty rests in Christ's most glorious humanity. To be " lost in God," for the Christian, is not to enter some mystic trance but to be rightly involved in community.

Relatedly, we must recover what salvation meant to the Hebrew. Wyclif, whose translation markedly precedes the Authorised Version, gets through the New Testament without ever using the word " salvation." The word he used, where salvation now occurs, was health. " This day health is come to thy house " is Wyclif's sufficient translation. Indeed, in the Song of Zaccharius at the beginning of St. Luke's Gospel, " knowledge of salvation " is translated " science of health." Salvation, for the Hebrew, is science of health. Wyclif is also interesting in his translation of the verb " glorify." Of all the words that our modern approach has ballooned up into

thin air, it is the word glory. " O that will be glory for me "
well conveys this etheric attitude. But a closer examination
of the word gives the condition for being able so to sing " on
the Other Side." For glory means *the manifestation of God
on earth*. Thus Wyclif frequently translates " to glorify " as " to
clarify " : to make God clear to men. A boy threw a stone
at the stained glass window of the Incarnation. It nicked out
the " E " in the word HIGHEST in the text, " GLORY TO
GOD IN THE HIGHEST." Thus, till unfortunately it was
mended, it read, " GLORY TO GOD IN THE HIGH ST."

At least the mended E might have been contrived on a swivel
so that in high wind it would have been impossible to see which
way it read. Such is the genius, and the offence, of the Christian
revelation. Holiness, salvation, glory are all come down to
earth in Jesus Christ our Lord. Truth is found in the constant
interaction of the claim that the apex of the Divine Majesty
is declared in Christ's Humanity. The Word of God cannot
be dissociated from the Action of God. As the blood courses
through the body, so the spiritual is alone kept healthy in its
interaction in the High Street. God's revelation of Himself
was not a series of mighty acts done *to* Israel but a series performed *in and through* Israel as a community in the totality
of its life.

THE OLD TESTAMENT DECLARES IT

Is not this interaction the rise and fall in the whole Bible ?

Through familiarity, we miss the shattering novelty of God's
revelation of Himself at Mount Sinai. Is it too much to say
that God there declared the only way you can have communion
with Him is in what you keep doing about your neighbour ?
" Communion with Me ? " says God, " don't steal, or lie,
or covet, or commit adultery." And you remember what
happened. The people winced! " Let's get back to Egypt,"
they murmured, " back to proper religion ! "

Through formalism, we miss, too, the continuance of this
offensive revelation when they reached the Promised Land.

They systematised the Ten Commandments in the Year of Jubilee. And the Year of Jubilee was not an affair of tents, with a big top marquee and a lot of little tents for publications, press and parsons, as one might associate with a religious revival. It was a redistribution of tents and of land such as one might associate with extremely unpopular social legislation. And it was what the Hebrews meant by Holiness. It was not a Jamboree where hearts were to be moved. It was a debt cancellation in which landmarks were not to be removed. (And I wonder what they make of it in Bible class in Kenya.) You remember what happened when the Year of Jubilee came round, and those who, through dissoluteness, had lost their plot, got it back; and those who had bought too many gave them up; that all might recover their dignity as persons? You remember what happened when every fifty years they were reminded of the kind of community in which God was interested? The people winced! They began seriously to develop " religion "; to elaborate it, expand it with priests and bullocks, doves and first-fruits, and above all scapegoats: so elaborating the Covenant that, while glorifying the principle, they might, by due ecclesiastical devotion, escape the practice.

It was of course the completeness of that escape that pressured forth the *social* prophets. Even to-day we retain the name in the hope of escaping the implication.

At the time that Isaiah wrote his " 58th Chapter " there was apparently a " Tell Israel " campaign in progress. Without an atom of charlatanry there were all sorts of retreats organised. They " sought God daily ": they delighted " to know His ways," they fasted, they made sacrifices, yet God did not seem to see or hear. " Why do we fast and Thou takest no knowledge? " they complained, as they opened their daily newspapers, full of the usual gloom, while they trundled back in their bullock wagons to their offices in the city after a perfect bean-feast of a revival. And God said to Isaiah, " Get hold of the largest possible loud speaker " (lift up thy voice like a trumpet) " and speak for Me saying, ' Is it such the fast that I have chosen?

. . . Is not this the fast that I have chosen ? to loose the bonds of wickedness, to let the oppressed go free, and that ye break every yoke ? Is it not to deal thy bread to the hungry, and that thou bring the poor that are cast out to thy house ? When thou seeest the naked that thou clothe him : and that thou hide not thyself from thine own flesh ? ' "

If only, God assures, men will return to the social contract then their religion will break into life. They will neither need revival or know times of spiritual death. " The Lord shall guide them continually and they shall be like a watered garden, and like a spring of water, whose waters fail not." They shall be called (Moffatt's translation) " the repairer of ruins, the restorer of wrecked homes."

If all this sounds a little offensive, it is well to remember the effect for Isaiah. Not only did they kill him but ordered that he be sawn asunder with blunt saws. In other words, the people winced. Mark Twain once remarked that what worried him about the Bible was not the bits he did not understand, but the bits he did understand.

Thus the social prophets continue to the end, while the elaboration of religious observances only gains force with man's continued endeavour to keep in with God and to escape the wince.

With superb artistry, the Old Testament closes with Malachi. That short book includes the passage so often to be heard in the prayers in revival tents pleading with God that He will " open the windows of heaven and pour out a blessing that there shall not be room enough to receive it." In the mission hall it means that God may bless the mission with a great response. But in Malachi ? Here is the context—" Return unto me," saith the Lord. " Wherein shall we return ? " " Stop robbing me," saith the Lord. " Bring ye the whole tithe into the store house and prove me now, herewith, if I will not open the windows of heaven . . . "

I have claimed that the whole rise and fall of the Old Testament could modernly be described as economic inherence in the kind of community in which God is interested. Authentic religious revival depends on obedience to the social contract. In the startling phrase of John MacMurray, " The great contribution of the Hebrew to religion was that he did away with it." Ongoing life is where we meet God : in what is recorded in the *Daily Express* just as much as in the Parish Magazine.

And when we come to the last man, the last of the Old Men, to John crying in absolute solitude " Prepare ye the way of the Lord " : " Prepare for the new Man and the new day " ; what are his conditions for recognising the Messiah ? With the Hebrew " knowledge of salvation " in his thought, with science of health in his mind, what techniques of " repentance " does he advise ? Every one of them is what would now be labelled economic—soldiers are to be content with their wages ; businessmen are not to exact more than their due, and— for the rest—if any man has two coats or two loaves of bread he is to give one of them away.

It is some such responsive consciousness that must contemporaneously be recovered if we are to hear aright the Word of the Lord for our day. For, when the fullness of time was come God sent His Son, born of a woman, born under the law. Once more the God revealed is the God concealed. God revealed Himself as human, and as the true functioning of total community, as it had been revealed in the law. He is the At One Ment between the Godhead and the true community, but not in any ethereal sense of an isolated worshipping community but of a total community of body and soul.

He cannot be found except in community nor can community be found except in Him.

The truth revealed in the body of Israel is now fulfilled, both as comfort and challenge, in the body of our Lord.

THE NEW TESTAMENT CONFIRMS IT

In his first sermon he makes direct reference to the Year of Jubilee as fulfilled in Him. In His choosing of the disciples, as the type of the new Israel, and His assurance that they alone can understand His words, He declares His word is unintelligible except in the setting of community. In His constant healing of bodies and feeding of multitudes, He is concerned for the bodies as for the souls of men. And He gives the key to how alone we can have Holy Communion. It is in the measure in which we share our bread. In the whole manner of His teaching ministry, namely that holiness is to be found in the encounters of daily life, He lifts every human contact into an eschatalogical dimension. The Carpenter who claims He is one with the Father elevates the workman's bench to the dimensions of an altar. In a drama whose heroes are shepherds and ploughmen, fishermen and taxgatherers, women looking for coins, fathers in bed with their children, pearl merchants and factors, beggars and kings, and whose villains are priests and experts in the law, there is exquisitely built up the human scene as the place of His abiding, and the Temple courts as the place of His tears. Albeit He hopes against hope to the end that the place of the divine majesty may recover the glory of the humanity.

When that hope fails, He dies outside what men had called the Holy City, outside " holiness " to create the new centre of holiness. He gives up the ghost and the veil of the temple is rent from top to bottom. We are left with the " clarification " of God in the face of Jesus Christ.

It is this body that rises and ascends. It is this body that will come again. In the meantime He is with us always in the mystery of His body the Church.

(Some reader may here protest " But surely this is not the heart of the Gospel ? " Of course it is not. But this is the body of the Gospel in which the heart of the Gospel—our fallen condition and God's answer in Christ—can alone be fully apprehended.)

It was still in this sense that the early Church conceived of holiness. Pentecost is not just a spiritual experience but a bodily one. If they had not for long " all things in common " at least they never lost the sense of total community and of reverence for bodies. They were deeply concerned for the

68

total welfare of each other, rather as a modern Jewish Orthodox community use their common purse not just to support a derelict with a ticket for soup but to set him up again in business. The general witness of pacifism by the early Church was probably supported not so much by our modern arguments but by the overwhelming sense that even the body of an enemy was the temple of the Holy Ghost. (Even sixty years after the Church allowed its members to bear arms, it decreed that anyone who actually shed blood in battle should abstain from the sacrament for four years.)

Such was the area of holiness till the Constantine compromise: when increasingly the totality collapsed. Christianity had become overnight officially recognised as the religion of a state with vastly rich landlords and vastly poor slaves: a state with wars on every frontier. What confusion here for the divine total community! No wonder the more earnest fled into the deserts of Egypt, there met the non-Christian mystics of the East, with their fear and detestation of the body, and began a recovery of a mystic way of holiness totally at variance with the unique Hebrew concept. Thus " religion " started again.

TRUE REVIVAL ALWAYS RECOVERS IT

Since then, in ways we need not trace, the ups and downs of the Church could be discerned as the up and down of this same strand. Martin of Tours was a recoverer. Finding a Church dissociate again from the eternal challenge, he sent out his groups of twelve, consisting of agriculturalists, teachers, musicians, fishermen as well as preachers, that Christ might be known as the Lord of all good life.

Francis of Assisi, choosing the dress for his Order as identical with that of the poorest field labourer, throwing out the doll from the crib at the Christmas Eve Service and placing there instead the crying child of an embarrassed mother; turning sun, fire and water into members of a human family; got the Highest and the High Street once more " gloriously " conjoined.

Rome was never satisfied with its attempts to balance the spheres of the temporal and the spiritual in complement: though it degenerated almost to contentment with " symbols " of totality in its monastic orders.

Geneva attempted a recovery with a common table and a fair linen cloth in place of a distant altar : Calvin busied himself with the dustbins of the city streets and the introduction of dentists, to bring back body to the Faith. Christian men busied themselves for centuries with the sacrament of wealth and the dangers of interest on capital.

NEMESIS

Till it all ran out into the divorce, between " holiness " and the " health services," which is our tragedy to-day.

To summarise the then and now, let us close with two quotations. Here speaks, first of all, the Church in one of its great days. Pope Gregory the Great, not a lunatic fringe man, but the instigator of the conversion of England, could write thus : " We must make men clearly understand that the land that yields men income is the common property of all men and its fruits for the common welfare. It is therefore absurd for people to think they are not robbers when they do not pass on what they have received to their neighbours. Absurd ! Because almost as many folk die daily as there are rations locked up for use at home. Really when we administer any necessities to the poor, we give them their own. We do not bestow our goods upon them, we do not fulfil the works of mercy. We discharge the debt of justice. What was given by a common God is only justly used when those who have received it use it in a common good." Such was the kidney of Gregory the Great : not a Dean of Canterbury but the instructor of Augustine, the first of that See. Such was the way *the Church* was expected to speak in his day. By God's grace, such criticism is largely outmoded in the internal economy of our land : but can we in our global environment to-day re-read that passage and refer it to the tension between West and East—

and not *wince* ? Almost " as many folk die daily " in the East as America " has rations locked up for use at home."

What matters here, however, is that such was the area of holiness then.

As second quotation, let the nineteenth century attitude be declared in the words of Thomas Chalmers. No pietist, he personally laboured more than any other in the Church in Scotland to relieve a brother's lot. Yet these are his words at the laying of the foundation stone of New College, Edinburgh : the new Divinity Hall of the Free Church that, a year before, had split away from the Establishment. The date is in the middle of the " hungry forties " when folk in the lowlands were wandering between Edinburgh and Glasgow eating raw carrots to keep body and soul together, their children sometimes dying by the roadside. New College abuts the Lawnmarket which at that time teemed with overcrowded citizens. No doubt they swarmed around the platform of the coming place of religious teaching, hoping that the New College might have something better to say about their plight than the Establishment had spoken. One wonders what they made of it when Chalmers, thus placed, said, " We leave to others the passions and politics of this world, and nothing will ever be taught, I trust, in any of our Halls, which shall have the remotest tendency to disturb the existing order of things, or to confound the ranks and distinctions which now obtain in society. But there is one quality between man and man which will be strenuously taught—the essential equality of human souls, and that in the high count and reckoning of eternity, the souls of the poorest of Nature's children, the raggedest boy who runs along the pavement, is of like estimation in the eyes of Heaven with that of the greatest and noblest in the land."

Thus spoke the leading exponent of the Faith in Scotland in the hungry forties. The divorce was complete.

One can, in fantasy, suppose that Karl Marx, reading the report of that speech in his London lodgings the next day, might with justice have remarked to his wife : " That finishes it. We must proceed to the emancipation of man without benefit of clergy."

If we are to answer Marx—which, in action, the Church has not yet begun to do—we will only understand what God is saying to us if, contemporaneous with our hearing, we are striving to become again the kind of community in which God is interested.

* * * *

POSTSCRIPT

At the conclusion of this lecture there gathered, unpremeditated, a somewhat animated group of Scots and Americans. It was not altogether a surprise that their criticisms, couched in the best of humours, crystallised under three heads: that while I had fairly summarised the prophetic element in the Bible, I had done scant justice to the priestly: that I had emphasised the Hebrew element in the New Testament and had disregarded the balance of the Greek element: and that I had implicity fallen for a " progressive " view of the significance of history. Lest any reader shares this sense of unbalance it may well be wisdom to indicate, without the details of argument, the line of my replies.

(a) Of course there is a place for the priestly element, as indeed it is developed in a later chapter, but is it not true of to-day, as of Bible times, that the priestly element is only justified in so far as it declares in the realm of worship the essential truth of the nature of God ? It is this truth that is so uniformly maintained by the prophets, and supremely conveyed in our Lord's own attitude both in conserving the eternal use of the Temple and in condemning its abuse. An article of priestly apparel is the stole. Just as all ecclesiastical vestments are a stylised form of a Roman citizen's ordinary apparel, so the ornate stole is the " vestigial remainder " of the sweat rag to dry the brow of a man in hot countries: carried sometimes over one shoulder, or circling the neck as a bather might to-day carry his towel. It may well have been His sweat rag

that Jesus used to dry the disciples' feet and indeed to wipe
from His brow in Gethsemane the blood that, in that great
intensity, His sweat had become. It is this symbol of service
and most costly obedience of which the stole is reminiscent.
The ultimate worship of God is what we do in the realm of
service or obedience in the market place. Ecclesiastical acts
of worship are absolutely necessary if we are to be inspired
to such service and capable of such obedience. Such obedience
is so beautiful in the eyes of God that we are right not to discount
the cultivation of beauty in worship. We must use every
assistance to adorn such acts of praise. But the moment we
are more interested in " dolling up the stole " than in being
inspired towards obedience, the priestly action ceases to
function for its intended purpose. " The house of prayer
for all nations " might degenerate again into " a den of thieves."
Practice fades without authentic worship, but practice can
be delayed by an absorption in its counterfeit. The prophetic
must constantly inform the priestly. Thus to exalt the prophetic
is not to discount the priestly but to fulfil it.

(b) Of the lack of the Greek element, in such concentration
on the Hebrew element in our Faith, it must suffice to say
we have so long emphasised the former that the latter should
have its day. For centuries we have been influenced, for
instance, by the Greek understanding of truth as an abstract
principle. For the Greek the " ideal," or the spiritual, was
not in the ongoing situation but hovering above men in its own
right : beckoning men forward " if haply they might find it "
and embrace it. But, too easily does truth become something
to come level with at some future date. Too rarely are we
faced, because of our Greek mood, with the urgency of immediate decision. " Certain Greeks came to the feast saying, ' Sir
we would see Jesus '." They were intrigued with His philosophy.
Perhaps they were about to argue with Him that, as His own
people obviously did not understand, there would be folk
in Athens who would thrill to His teaching. " Now is my
soul troubled and what shall I say," said Jesus, " Father save

F   73

me from this hour." But "except a grain of wheat fall into the ground and die, it abideth by itself alone. If it die it beareth much fruit." For the Hebrew, God's name is "Now"; "I am that I am." "This is the day of salvation." This is where the Cross comes to life. The immediate decision, the immediate obedience is what is sheer folly to the Greeks. It is because we so constantly evade it, rationalise and philosophise the truth that so often our pronouncements are so bold and our preambles so inordinately long and our record of actions so anaemic. The Greek element has brought us to our present decrepitude. The Hebrew element should have its chance. If it were given its prominence for a quarter of a century, in the general witness of the Church, it might revolutionise our world.

(c) But—to answer the third point—no one can plot the result of such a recovery. The third criticism was that I had fallen for a progressive view of the significance of history, for the old liberal view that it was the task of the Church to assist society to its next stage of development. Such a view is by no means necessary to the case. The revolution that would occur if the Church concentrated on action, in obedience to the Cross, might just as easily lead to its crucifixion as to its popular acceptance.

Around a thousand A.D., when the whole Church consciousness looked forward to the possible end of the world, in literal interpretation of the prophecies of Daniel, one might reasonably have expected a great Church passivity. Where was the point of outward action if at any moment Christ might come again in final judgment? Yet in fact there was a great upsurge of Church activity. What was that activity but the start of the building of the great cathedrals? Why so strange an action in such a mood? *So that Jesus, if He came, might have a beautiful place to come to . . . should He come to Milan, or Chartres, or Glasgow!* God's demands in our modern day are not to build great cathedrals. His possible temple is in living stones: a great harmony of people across the world in united praise. Whether

74

His coming again is distant or near should make no difference to our social zeal. We must labour now so that, if suddenly He came, there would be a more beautiful Africa, a lovely Gorbals, a more comely East Harlem for His advent! If He delays His coming then no limit should be placed on the power of the resurrection to transform our world even in its present dispensation. If all churchmen seriously moved again towards total community a revolution might indeed be accomplished as powerful and more lasting than anything communism has achieved. But this is not the motive of our concern for the social contract. Our motive is that God wills total community, and approximation towards it is an obligation of our communion with Him. For the rest " it is not for us to know times or seasons, which the Father hath set within His own authority."

CHAPTER FIVE

CHRIST AS PROPHET
IN THE MIDST OF THE CONGREGATION

In the two preceding lectures we have sought to recover the vision of " Him with whom we have to do " : and to envisage the nature of the environment in which we are alone likely to see Him. The glorious humanity of Christ, which is the apex of the Divine Majesty, cannot be conveyed in images however correct but can only be felt in the ongoing experience of a fellowship. This fellowship, we further saw, was an all embracing one rather than the " religious " fellowship which occurs to most minds when they think of " the Church." The reason the disciples would understand what Jesus was saying, while those outside would not, was because they were part of this wider fellowship.

It follows that in our contemporary situation essential to the " hearing " of the Word is the recovery of a congregation that begins again to fulfil the outlines of an all-embracing covenant. So long as the Church continues to think of itself as mainly a worshipping community, a " religious " community in the sense that the social prophets would have condemned, we are not likely truly to " hear." And as we look at the Church in which we are set, this child of the divorce that has been set up, we may indeed be despondent of recovery.

TO WHOM SHALL WE GO ?

Men can—and do—in their despondency contemplate joining the Roman branch of the Church, which at least has a political scheme interlaced with its splendid apparatus of worship: a whole complex world sociology locked away in cold storage with every kind of ecclesiastical trimming attached. But the nemesis of the Priest Workers turns us away from that. Or, more comprehensively, the witness, say in Spain, of what happens when they do recover a theocracy over the whole of life, cools us down.

Alternatively, in revolt from so grandiose a solution, we can contemplate joining so sincere an experiment in Christian living as the Bruderhof. Such is a community of married folk—hundreds of them—living out an all-embracing community, renouncing alike the capitalist and the communist way of life, with their own schools, their central farm, their moving central sacrament of the breaking of bread. Inside, so to say, a high stockade they live a hard life of true devotion, turning away from too close a view of the enormities of our fallen world. But, if such committed people will forgive the phrase, the lack-lustre of their eyes makes us pause.

Outside their stockade, they say, " there is no salvation." But they in turn forget that " outside the Cross there is no Church." By escaping the challenge of contemporary history, they largely escape the confrontation of the Cross.

Thus we are driven back to our contention that, in the collapse of Christendom, somehow the local congregation must move towards the recovery of a total community. Then we might begin to hear again what God is saying to the kind of community in which He is interested. By the terms of our thesis, this consciousness can come alive again only in the day to day work, the week to week worship, and the month to month outward concern of the local congregation. This confines us to pedestrian considerations indeed, if we are to be honest about our real condition. But our vision as we walk must be as constant as our pace may seem slow. We must keep direction, however cumbersome the briars on our path. Thus the three ensuing lectures seek to keep the vision and the facts together. Christ as Prophet, Priest and King—all titles of the Son of God in His most glorious humanity—must constantly be with us in the evolving " be-truth-al."

CHRIST AS PROPHET, PRIEST AND KING

Before we deal with Christ as Prophet in the day to day

work of the congregation, let us see this trinity of ministry correlated. Christ is in the Holy of Holies, at the heart of the Father, but He is in the midst of us always to the end of the world. We are the body of Christ in the world. Or we might say we are Judah in the court of the priests while the world outside is Israel whom He would win through us.

It is important to see the whole striving mass of the world of men as blindly looking for that which we have.

The furious activity of fallen mankind might be called the frustrated efforts of the human race to convince themselves that they are what they were meant to be: prophets, priests and kings! For you could say of that symbolic first man, Adam before the Fall, that he was fully prophet, priest and king. He was *prophet* in that he knew the meaning of things— God brought creation to him to be named: *priest* in that he perpetually walked with God; *king* in that he was lord of the elemental kingdom of beast and herb. Thus, of the human race, the sons of Adam, it could be said that they have the broken marks of their father. Their restlessness is that they cannot attain, their passion is to recover, their lost dominion.

Is this just words? Rather is there anything more actual than this conjoined glory and pathos of the human race? Here we are, if you care to put it so, in mid-twentieth-century still gamely talking of a possible United Nations: despite the whole long history of man's abject failure to approximate any such thing for century upon century! Here we are at it again as if to-morrow's papers might open golden gates of disarmament and trust! This is not just true of churchmen but of the whole sentient race. What pathos! Why has man not committed suicide long ago? Is there a rational answer except in the glory and everlasting hope that also forever reverberates in his make up? The restlessness of the fallen sons of Adam is that they cannot attain, but their passion remains to recover, their lost dominion. There is no accounting for the paradox otherwise. In their intellects they still have the instinct of *prophecy*. What motivates the so-called secular sociologist but to know the result or outcome of varying combinations in the affairs of men ? What is that but the broken vestige of his prophecy ? In their consciences they have the thirst for right relations, for justice in the outward parts, for righteousness in the inward parts—the groping of their spirits after personal peace. What is that but the broken vestige of their *priesthood*, inherited and defaced ? And, in their wills, what thirst for kingship ! With what constancy they search for power, with what grimace of disappointment do they spit it out, horrified at the bitter taste when they have given a lifetime to obtain it : seeking dominion because kingship belongs to them, yet forever denied it. What is that but the broken vestige of man's sovereignty ?

Thus the world outside is not a conglomeration. It is Israel, God's dear ones and His lost. We do not have to teach them a new language to understand us. We have only to be the new Judah, in whom the lost prophecy, the lost priesthood and the lost kingship are manifest again.

And we are coming to a new fullness of the time. The dreams of sociologists degenerate to a nightmare : and they know it. Men's striving after righteousness leads but to vanity and everywhere men begin to cry, " Who shall deliver us from the body of this death ? " In our unified world, our close knit cities, our interlaced trades and professions, men's myriad determinations to dominate begin dangerously to collide and, as in Israel of old, an authoritarian cry is heard, " Give us a king " : be it sovereignty of nation, business monopoly or trade union amalgamation.

Only in Christ is the redemption of the threefold tragedy of man : a full-blooded redemption indeed. No " pale Galilean " is He, calling men off from this tremendous hunt. Thus we must not strain off His tremendous offer into a rarefied spirituality for the pallid and the partial. Christ the Prophet forever offers us the true pattern of community. As Priest He offers the righteousness for which we strive. Finally by our obedience to that pattern, our acceptance of that righteousness, He offers us freedom. " Whom to serve is perfect freedom " runs the collect. But it is more lucid in the Latin, " *Quem Servire*

regnare est : whom to serve as a slave is to reign as a king.''
No pale Galilean is He. Not only does He lead captivity captive, He gives gifts unto men.

THE THREEFOLD ASPECT OF HIS PROPHECY

It is in this total perspective that we now move to consider Christ as Prophet in the midst of the congregation.

This aspect of His redemptive work is of three kinds. He was, in His own person, the final revealer of the nature of God : consequent on that a community, best described as a family, is required, in which this relationship can be conveyed and exercised.

He was, secondly as prophet, the predictor of final judgment, assuring us of the permanency of this community and the ultimate destruction of all communities that fall short of that family. Consequently the congregation must carry in its life an inherent judgment on all lesser communities.

He was, thirdly, prophet of a new heaven and a new earth, wherein dwell right relations. In consequence we are empowered to be steadfast, always abounding in the work of the Lord, for our labour towards community is not in vain, as community is our final destination.

Now that Christ is ascended, He perpetuates this prophetic work through the Church. He is with us always, in the midst of the congregation as patterner, encourager of community and constant comfort. In Him we must portray the life of the forgiving family confident of its validation at the last and thereby challenging the lesser communities in which it is set.

We are, in what we write *by our life together*, the only " epistles " that men outside now read. Only as they see a prophetic Church will sociologists think it worth while to read the epistles again, as more significant than the day dreams of a Mumford.

COME DOWN A KEY

To descend to practicalities is no more than to adopt the

method of St. Paul. He always " started with mysticism and
ended with politics " : proving, beyond a peradventure, for
instance, that it was unthinkable for a Christian to accept
slavery . . . and then giving instructions how slaves should be
treated! We must come down a key.

I can imagine some reader scanning with growing amazement
the preceding paragraphs and being tempted to say " Is the
author of this book really supposing that he is describing *our*
local congregation, St. Andrew's-on-the-Rocks ? " Actually I
am : nor need you get depressed. St. Paul when he came
down from his sublimities apparently had to write of porno-
graphy and bestiality continuing among his people and standing
somewhat in the way of their achieving their true vocation.
We have made some progress in our day!

What, then, are we going to do, in our church halls, to
begin to convey the fuller vision ? Remember it is the weekday
life in the " small hall " rather than our extravagant offers
from the soap box oration that will challenge men outside.
Our powerful words outside will lose edge if, convicted, the
urgent enquirer comes in . . . only to find us engaged in a
whist drive. (This is even more true if there are only fifty-one
cards in the pack—as seems to happen in a church hall as
nowhere else on earth—the three of hearts having been purloined
by the earlier restless activity of the Brownie pack, those
" little flowers of St. Vitus ".)

Never forget that in no previous age has the church hall
been so dissociated from " total " concern. Even the nineteenth
century congregation (which had no church halls) had a better
chance. For " Scotland " was still the church hall. The
Church, very often literally, was right beside the market-
place. Through open church windows the Word reverberated
into the total life of the town, with a response, say, in honest
market dealings. Each week thousands of pounds changed
hands without paper-accounting at all. Woe betide the farmer
who in those days went back on a mere nod given in the local
tavern, if later a better price came up. He had to leave the

district. That is, society was responsive to the Church's Word. Scotland was the church hall. Or, in the Sabbath observance controversy, in one Presbytery in the mid-nineteenth century, a minister spoke for four hours and continued his speech at the next day's diet. The secular press carried his speech in four columns. Too often, to-day, the press report us only when something goes wrong, but then all Scotland was the listening community to the Church's Word.

Do not forget either, that, alongside the formed community of interaction, there was in those days a uniform word to be spoken, a unity of standard, a common confession.

To-day Scotland's social life is independent of its Church: Scotland is not listening. Nor, if they were, would we have a common word to say. How onerous is our task.

LET US BE PERSONAL

Can we approach it in personal terms ? If this emerges at first as almost cynical, this is only designed to give confidence to the reader that we deal with the real situation.

Consider a young man, his assistantship over, now nominated to his first charge. He has no formed word to declare : a dash of Emil Brunner saying " ja," of Karl Barth saying " nein," and of most of his teachers saying " let 'em all come." He has the disturbing memory of a theological debate where he voted with those who claimed we should now return to adult baptism, owing to difficulties of infant baptism in a " missionary " situation : disturbing because he is now going to have to dissemble before the Lord for the rest of his ministry by baptising infants ! He has been to a Keswick convention and has returned transfigured with a glow. He has been to Iona and has returned transmogrified as by a blow. He has sought clarity from a " balanced man " who has assured him that both positions are tenable, but who has no time to explain as he must catch a train for Wick. He is as convinced that all Christians should take a responsible part in politics as he is aware that he has never done so. Secretly, perhaps he would admit that, despite his membership in the Student Christian Movement and his leadership of the youth group in his own church, the most rounded fellowship he has known was in the football team of his school and in the drama group in which he played lead.

Rather desperately he had tried, at the end of his course, to get a Continental scholarship not because he was consumed to know what Bultmann meant, but to " demythologise " his own collective experience to date.

He is at sixes and sevens. Humanly speaking he has but three instruments, his Bible, his personality—built as above—and his father's old writing desk. Yet in a few weeks he is to preach, to lead worship, and to serve in the same congregation day by day and week by week for at least the next five years.

He has made perhaps only two clear decisions. He is not going to play football or get mixed in dramatics—the two areas where he once felt the fullness of life.

He has not been with this congregation for long, however, before he grasps that he is at least in a community of suffering. If he is at sixes and sevens he finds his congregation at twelves and fourteens in its weekday life.

There is, at first sight, what can only be described as a collectivity of persons. Let us focus the problem by a look at the Kirk Session : which must serve in our analysis as a micro-cosm of the congregation, as indeed it is. Elders can be divided into three groups—the marvellous, the mediocre and the morose.

He will not have been there long before he disconcertingly discovers that the marvellous are not confined to those who have had some radiant experience of personal conversion. Such of course are among them. But there is the doctor who by his training is even suspicious of such an experience : but he is pure gold. There is, too, the electrician who spends hours on church fabric but has never been present at a Holy Week service. There is the man who never utters at the prayer meeting for the sufficient reason that he has never been there but who, without thought of recompense, rose at five every

Sunday morning to put on the furnaces for the beadle who had a six months illness.

Now all these are constant in church-attendance and with different personality serve their districts costingly. Dare we say of the electrician " the gift of knowledge," of the doctor " the gift of wisdom," and of the evangelical " the gift of faith " ? At least we cannot deny that all these are part of the marvellous Body.

Secondly in the eldership—and as microcosm of the whole—are the mediocre. As men outside they are sterling, human, responsive and free, and no doubt for these reasons were chosen. But somehow, at a Session meeting they go dumb with a dumbness that has to be heard to be believed. I have no doubt of the reason why they go sessionally dumb. They are consumed by a sense of inferiority because they have never been converted and feel therefore counterfeit in an assembly of God. We shall return to them. Finally there are the morose, who can be calculated to obstruct every glad occasion. They are not only morose as elders. They are morose as men. Always there is a reason if you can find it: like the one who cut in half every suggestion for advance that the minister made. Was it a mission ? Then let it be in the hall and not the church. Was it new lighting ? Then let it be in the church but not the hall. He was a retired man and all was explained when it was discovered that he had been in insurance, spending all his life in the claims department. To these also we shall return, as they have brought many a young minister in sorrow, if not to the grave at least to the committee for the transference of ministers. Such then is the collectivity. And as the elders, for brevity, have stood for the people so let two organisations represent the galaxy of organisations that make the hall to shine from seven to eleven six days a week, in cataclysmic variety.

There is the Woman's Guild. Flourishing where there is not a Rural Institute, kept alive by a not dissimilar programme, it withers to a duller tone where specifically religious activities are attempted. Albeit it makes a dutiful showing at the Women's

Day of Prayer : and is sincerely interested when the missionary comes along. But the zenith of its year is the Burns Supper. Then every household pours forth its napery, crockery and cutlery in a holocaust of offering. For an evening of glorious release there is a verisimilitude of Pentecost : a flashing resurgence of " all things in common."

(I do not ask the reader whether this description is acceptable : I only ask whether it is not too often true.)

As other type of the existence of community I choose the Boys' Brigade. Its vaulting horse disfigures the passage and defies the byelaws of clear exit in the event of fire. But what a remarkable consistency of community it achieves, with its Bible open at the centre of the fellowship, its physical fulfilment, its intellectual assistances, its passionate loyalties. To which must, significantly, be added its paradoxical problem : the amazing paucity of its membership who ultimately emerge in the full fellowship of the Church.

FACING THE FACTS

Now what are we to make of this collectivity of folk, of these vestiges of full community ?

After about six months our young minister sees an alternative choice. On the one hand he is tempted to conclude that Christ as Prophet is not enough in the midst of this congregation. He proceeds to the cliché too often heard—" the trouble is there are not enough proper Christians in this congregation "— and devises a programme calculated to give the pre-eminence to what is called " the spiritual." That this course greatly lessens numbers does not, and should not, disturb. What is disturbing is the coldness of that pure gold doctor, the departure of the electrician, and somehow no one left to put on the furnace when the beadle is ill. The mediocre, no longer dumb with apprehension, are seized of a paroxysm of fear. They always knew this was religion ; and now it is coming to them. The Woman's Guild dwindle to a moiety, gamely accepting the new spiritual emphasis. But, denied a Burns celebration they maddeningly transfer and continue to proffer their pentecostal offerings at the secular Co-operative Guild. The morose merely transfer their lugubriety. Having previously obstructed that there was no religion in the fellowship, they now complain there is no life in the church hall.

If, of grace, the young minister resiles from this solution—having seen its effect in the neighbouring parish—he is apt to accept the continuing pandemonium. But he re-opens the works of Reinhold Niebuhr: for was it not he who wrote that there must be a tension between the sacred and the secular ? Can he not therefore infuse into the ongoing situation certain eternal truths of life that will manifest the Godhead and give order to the chaos ? He painfully concocts an address to the Session that he feels, on his way to the meeting, is probably the ablest condensation of Niebuhr's position ever placed before the non-theological mind. After an impassioned delivery there is a pause reminiscent of a Quaker session but doubtfully filled with a comparable content. One of the marvellous then asserts it should be put in print and distributed: one of the mediocre asks why throughout he pronounced *neighbour* in such a peculiar way: while a morose asks what, if anything, is to be done about the Boys' Brigade camp-account which was considered at the last meeting. A subject of patent interest having been recovered, the marvellous do battle with the morose while the mediocre remain sessionally dumb.

Our minister, finding that at least his own account of Niebuhr doesn't work in the actual situation, transfers—almost unconsciously—the tension to his inner mind: playing a mental game of tennis as he swings the dialectic of everything from the secular to the sacred court, and back, in his imagination, endangering a crick in his intellectual neck but endangering nothing else at all: himself neither noticeably more sacred nor more committed to the secular.

In the congregation, the mixture is much as it was before.

ADVENT

Is there no third way ? Or, at least, is there not a method of more simply approaching the second choice ? Is there no way to begin the recovery of that " involved " Congregation by which alone our modern world is to be challenged ? There is. To dramatise it let us claim that there is one religious occasion when the whole body of the congregation do come together, the marvellous, morose and mediocre, the Burns night specialists and the vaulting-horse enthusiasts, together with half the house of Israel from the outer courts.

The occasion is the midnight Christmas Eve service.

Here there flashes before you, probably more than at any sacrament, however disturbing be the fact, the true Body of Christ. For what does Christmas say to us here ? At least it reminds us that God reveals Himself in many ways. At Bethlehem Jesus was not just revealed to the devout. He was revealed to the shepherds who were doing their work in the field. He was revealed to the wise men who were led, not by the Bible but by their own examination of truth, to the cradle by a star : having themselves grown tired of trying to be clever. Only thirdly, in point of time, though equally significantly, He was revealed to the devout in the temple courts who were " looking for the consolation of Israel." What do we deduce ? We are recalled to the truth that the community from which we must start is the community which God has given us : with Christ in the midst.

The man who cleans those furnaces, though he never attends a prayer meeting, is a shepherd to whom God has revealed Himself. His devotion is to the Way. The doctor or teacher who never come to Holy Week services are the modern wise men : Their devotion is to truth—and all that is true is of God. The evangelicals who can give chapter and verse, who love the temple courts, are quite essential as interpreters of what is happening in the midst of the congregation. They are the devout, though like Simeon and Anna they are often old.

THE WHOLE PEOPLE OF GOD

If this truth of the "whole people of God" can break through into the consciousness of all, the true life of the congregation begins to pulsate. The spiritual courses through the whole body. The blood of the redemption begins to flow.

What treasures the wise men begin to bring: gold and frankincense and myrrh. The erstwhile workaday mediocrities cease, like the shepherds, to be afraid. The Gospel is something they can understand, for it starts about a Baby and they have always been quite certain that babies are holy anyway. Even the tongues of the dumb in the session begin to sing. And just as surely as we must believe that somehow, on the first Christmas, shepherds, wise men and devout must have got together, if only for a night in a cellar like some pristine resistance movement, so triangular interaction and enrichment begin between their modern counterparts. You can almost hear the stiffened joints of the body ecclesiastical, warmed of the Spirit, being massaged into conscious semblance again of the kind of community in which God is interested: of the mystic human body of our Lord. This diversity of unity begins to seep into the whole life of the congregation.

In visiting the shepherds now you do not wait in awful silence to hear them mouth religious phrases as proof of their membership nor do you dismiss as small talk their plain words. In every activity of living, in all the holiness of their care for children, in the toys they make and the sacrifices they undergo for them, you have heavenly conversation.

In visitation of the wise men you do not make sectional appeal that they come to the Holy Week services. You hear from them the marvels of their sciences not as noises off but as evidence of the living God. So that whether it be the great constellations or flowers in the crannied wall that is their interest, your engaged attention will bring them to know, with you, that all these are the garments of the living God. Shot through every interest is the Divine Majesty who did not disdain to inhabit His own creation that one day all might be redeemed to Him. For this is the question your wise men and shepherds are really asking us—

" *How far above the things of earth is Christ at God's right hand ?*
How far above yon snowy peaks do His white angels stand ?
Must we fare forth to seek a world beyond that silent star ?
Forsake these dear familiar homes and climb the heights: how far ?"

And this should be our reply to them : How far ?

" *As far as meaning is from speech; as beauty from a rose.*
As far as music is from sound: and poetry from prose.
As far as love from friendship is: as reason is from truth.
As far as laughter is from joy: and early years from youth.
As far as love from shining eyes; as passion from a kiss.
So far is God from God's green earth: so far that world from this."*

The apex of the divine majesty is in His most glorious humanity.

The so-called secularities of the Woman's Guild become touched with the light of the shekinah. The shared accoutrements of the Burns Supper, and all its banter, become occasions not for your disdaining but for your interpreting. Broken pottery though it be, it lies at hand for your assembling. And that awkward vaulting-horse in the passage of the Boys' Brigade should sometimes be set beside the Holy Table in your church that a sermon may be preached from the text, " We pray God your whole spirit and soul and body be preserved, entire and without blame, at the coming of the Lord Jesus " : when in a body He shall visit the earth and come among us to reign in a new heaven and a new earth where right relations dwell. Unless our young minister is very careful he will find himself playing football again and leading the dramatic club: so little afraid will he now be to appear as human.

It is Christ the Prophet in the midst of the congregation who inspires us to this first fruit of community—this response

---

*By the late Rev. G. A. Studdert Kennedy: founder of the Industrial Christian Fellowship.

to the Fatherhood of God which He revealed—unripe or bruised though that fruit may at present be.

But the necessity of two additions will soon appear. We have spoken of a plethora of organisations. Is it the departmentalism, in all aspects of social life, that has severed into " age groups " the life of the average congregation ? One necessity is the recovery of the " Parish Meeting "—it might be in place of the shrivelled " evening service." A place must be found for the intermingling of shepherds, wise men and devout : and the mixing of the wise devout with the brash young shepherds. Here must be brought to discussion every department of man's living. The electrician to speak of his work, the doctor of his science, and the devout of their interpretations. Here can be nurtured back into the consciousness of the people the whole secular prose of life that, with God, can be turned into poetry : the whole reasoning of local " politics " that only God can elevate into truth. The housing of the district will bring a marvellous contribution from the shepherds—who know it as no sociologist has ever plumbed. The delinquent problem of the town will be spoken of by the doctor as no parent has envisaged it, and by the parent as no Commission has grasped. In such organic meeting the parrot word of the evangelical is stilled, but the true word of the evangelical is called forth in relevance and in power.

Our point here may be clarified by an Army parallel. In the First World War, the chaplain was responsible for the football team, the concert party, the officers' mess accounts, the domestic embroilments at home of the young soldier who was disintegrating—so that he spoke on Sunday to a fellowship with which by many ties he was identified. Such is the organisation of the army to-day that all the secular issues have been withdrawn from his domain : " that he may confine himself to the spiritual." The fine intention usually results in his being the one man with his collar reversed. Again, I once visited a prison where an instruction was exhibited—admittedly yellow with age. In effect it said I was not to converse with the prisoner, about his case, his past, his family or his future but was to confine myself to " spiritual subjects." How, in Bible terms, can you divorce a prisoner's soul from his case, his family or his future ? I broke the regulations in the name of God.

It is an incarnate Word, clothed in the flesh of the ongoing environment, that must be spoken.

THE NEW FAMILY

But a related addition is necessitated. It is the Rev. Ernest Southcott, of the Church of England at Leeds, who has ventured furthest here. In essence he discovered that the " rounded " congregation did not come to his Parish Meeting. Most felt it was meant for the devout, praying for its success provided they were not asked to share in its achievement. So Southcott went out, with a leaf from the Priest Workers notebook in Paris, into the very different environment of a housing estate. In the homes of his people he gathered groups from his congregation. There they discussed everything that was coming. There too he baptised the children, after full instructions to the parents, reverently assisted by " the street " : both members and interested invited guests. Sometimes seven times a day he dispenses the Sacrament of Holy Communion at the family altar—the bread being taken from the family loaf for the great interpretation. His latest exciting problem is the ecumenical nature of those who press in for so solemn yet familiar a feast. At the crowded family meal that ensues every subject comes up for discussion in the afterglow of the eternal moment : the problems of the " street " are brought under the judgment of God.

It is in such gatherings, congregational or domestic, that Bible-study breaks into life. And as Bible prophecy is always the Word/Act conjoined, another leaf can be taken from the remarkable Jocist Movement of the Roman Church, by which a group can be instructed to " see, judge and act " on innumerable local situations in the light of the Word. Either from parish meeting or from home altars, it is not long before groups go out to mend housing, to create playing fields, and to heal the sick. It is not long before a mutual economic witness becomes the centre of discussion : embryo and halting but prophetic of a Church that will not be content with the vision of His glorious humanity till it recovers the modern meaning of " all things in common " with which to challenge the fallen communities of men.

LESSER COMMUNITIES ARE CHALLENGED

This " all in " family, beginning to go " all out," has of course to confront the lesser communities of the world—the Rotary, the Co-operative Guild, the Lawn Tennis Club and the Drama Group, etc.—with an even more central Word of our Gospel. And here, incidentally, we begin to grasp what to do with the " morose." This " all in " family must be the forgiving society. Here indeed it becomes prophetic and unique. In explanation I would claim that the most Christian congregation I have ever met are outwith the organisation of the Church. They call themselves " Alcoholics Anonymous." They might be called " the total community of the late morose." None can join who has not been an inebriate. All have known themselves to be in durance vile. Enquirers lurch in and out to find a brotherhood—and sisterhood—that dare not patronise and are content to love and patiently to wait.

I have been rung up on the telephone—because I am proud to belong to a Community House that gives them meeting room—by an inebriate with two hundred convictions with whom they were still as patient as I was not. He said he was " at it again in X street and nothing could stop him now unless A.A. found him before he became unconscious." Within an hour four members had left their different places of business and were weaving their way through every pub in X street till they saved their man. (I could not help wondering how many members of such congregations as I have served would have rung me up to get the congregation to rescue them in the moment of their sin.) Here is a body/soul fellowship whose power is their admission that they are all—together—

sinners. What holds them is a common need. What heals them is the patient fellowship of this admission. I have sat in a small group of them while they argued for four hours with one of their members who was courageously asserting his determination to go out from amongst them : the devil being then in charge. And, though no prayer was said, Christ walked in the midst of that little congregation so that His very breath was hot upon one's cheek.

APOSTOLICS ANONYMOUS

The Church, the local fellowship, must become " Apostolics Anonymous " again. Who are our " morose " but those who are inebriate with pride : inheritors, it may well be, of a home that mismanaged them in youth in its infidelity or spiritual debauch. And why do they remain morose in the midst of us ? or why, when a church member " blots his copy book " and goes to prison, do we—like as not—plot how to set him up again *in another town* ? Because we ourselves will not give up the pint-pots of our malice and the high-charged barrels of our self-esteem. (Even as I write these words, cogent though they be, I am pleased with their artistry and design. We are none of us righteous, no not one. " All our righteousnesses are as filthy rags.") We will not admit we are in like condition : that we are constant thieves of God's time, if of nothing else.

The new humility will never be recovered save in a body that is really human, that can laugh at its failures and admit its ignorance. It is a fellowship such as this that begins to be spoken of in the criminal quarters of our towns as something worth looking into. (And, to judge by St. Paul's lists of the sins from which the members had departed, it must have been among those quarters that the early Church also had a reputation.) It is such a fellowship that might even attract the attention of Teddy Boys, that is those who are the difficult among them : though one wonders why all of them are suspected of nefarious practices when most of them do no more than imitate the dress that the West End invented and adopts.

93

And, by the same token, it is a fellowship that holds such as these that begins to be spoken of as not quite respectable, a little too broad and somewhat dangerous to join.

But such was always the mark of a living Church.

Thus there would begin to be manifest the embryo of a family which, by its costly forgiveness, challenges all the lesser moral fellowships of men. Forgiveness is a foolishness that disturbs men—yet it is the lack of it which, even before our eyes, is likely to bring our civilisation crashing to the ground.

Such a family is always in upheaval: the upheaval of risking love. Nothing is ever neat about it. But Christ is in the midst assuring us that the end is none other than a community of love: for which all these endeavours are but a school.

Bernanos, the great French, loving critic of the Church, has a daring picture of the Bride of Christ as the farmer's wife! He visits the farm and finds all in disarray: there are the workers to be given breakfast at five, the children to be got up and fed for school, the farmer returning around 9 for his own full breakfast, the milk pails to be scalded, the big mid-day dinner, the children returning hungry at 6, the darning to be done, the letter to be written to the absent son, and the early bed: to be ready for it to start again next day at 5. The kitchen and the farmyard seem in perpetual disarray. Could it not be neater? he asks. . . . Later, he returns to the same farm. The children are crying. The farmer is broken. The workers are querulous. The yard is derelict. The kitchen is chaotic. Why? Because the farmer's wife has died.

The living Church, though never neat, keeps God's world from complete disaster.

And, if hard words occasionally have been spoken here, do not forget that the present Church, as it is with all its praise and blame, is out and away the most active community in our land. Compared with those active in all the political parties put together, the Church's active membership is as one hundred to one. It has a record of weekly attendance that no trades union or trade association can begin to approximate. Everywhere the new ferment is bubbling up. It is alive because Christ is in the midst. If we more recover His full ministry of prophecy we can, even with her present numbers, revolutionise our land. In the meantime we must remain steadfast in the upheaval, always abounding in the work of the Lord, for our labour is not in vain in the Lord.

*　*　*　*

POSTSCRIPT

At the close of this lecture Professor Norman Porteous, of the Department of Old Testament Studies, came into the anteroom and said, " If what you say is true, George, it indicates the need for an experiment in a new kind of Divinity Hall." I replied, " That remark is better to come from you than from me, Norman." At which point another listener entered and said, " I quite agree : what is wanted is more classes in sociology and psychology as well as the usual disciplines." Professor Porteous and I, after recovering balance, both spoke simultaneously in almost exactly similar terms. Such was precisely—we chimed in—what was *not* wanted. Sociology and psychology, yes, but they must not be tagged on to swell the curriculum but somehow interlaced in the ongoing theological revelation. We further agreed that it could be no more than a tentative experiment. It would be the height of irresponsibility to pretend that we yet knew its outline, and of ungraciousness to convey that the present development in the normal Divinity Halls is not attempting to meet the situation. But the issue remains whether, in our present situation, we can ever make the grade by getting the intellectual concepts clear and then asking men to embark on the " be-truthal." Presently the Church of Scotland requires about a hundred new ministers a year to keep us level with our needs. This takes no account of an increasing population and of the growing number of specialist appointments that absorb some who previously went into parish work. To meet this need, in recent years, never more than fifty have become qualified. Should this continue, a major crisis will be upon us in a decade.

In such a plight is it a hopeless dream to conjecture a small fifth wheel appended—experimentally—to our coach : the four present Divinity Halls ? Entrants for it would certainly be required to take a prior arts degree : intellectual standard is the last thing to be discounted. But, to give reins to fancy, would it be an impossible thing to plot, in co-operation with the Committee for the Education of the Ministry, a new divinity curriculum, centred in a new locus ?

Among its necessities might be—living together in community with chores as part of the pattern, a first year covering the main aspects of the present four disciplines : a long summer spent as labourers in heavy industry without classes : a winter spent in community in a large city parish with complete involvement in its activities, its visiting, its youth clubs with but one lecture a day : a final year in withdrawal from parish and industry with a major concern for theology, for the devotional life, and for pastoral training, in light of that experience. That final year would be devoid of formal examinations but not of formal assessment by other means. It might not appeal to the scholar—for whom ample provision is already normally made—but might it not appeal to many young men who are committed Christians, have not the capacities of a scholar, but might ultimately give yeoman service to the ministry ? Are we quite certain that their equipment would, at the end of such a course, be inferior to some presently in our Halls who, equally, have not the capacities of a scholar but, perforce, must attempt its verisimilitude ? Are we quite certain that such men, indeed, would not be better equipped for the peculiar demands of our day ? Indeed are we sure there are not also men of first-class scholastic attainment who might rather choose some such approach for the needs of our time ? The staff of such an experiment should be men of the highest intellectual calibre. But two other qualifications would also be desirable—that they had themselves ministered in a city charge and that they would be prepared to return to parish work after five years and make way for a new staff.

CHAPTER SIX

CHRIST AS HIGH PRIEST
IN THE MIDST OF THE CONGREGATION

Two artificialities are incumbent in this chapter. By the terms of our thesis the work cannot be divorced from the worship, nor the person from the community. Thus, all that is written here about worship must be trellised in the mind, with the concept of a working congregation as it is portrayed in the last chapter. Again, personal devotion, without which all corporate worship becomes formal, is the subject of our final chapter. Its necessity must also be taken for granted in what is our present interest. Here we are concerned with the worship of the congregation. If it is only in a full-blooded congregation that the heart of the Gospel can beat freely, it is in its corporate worship that the Gospel is made to circulate to every extremity of work. Worship is that covenant exercise which has the constant two-way traffic of angels descending and ascending. It is that exercise in true being whereby our prophetic ministry is cleansed and renewed.

In this chapter our task is twofold. First it is to recover our vision of the High Priesthood of Christ, with still in His hands the mark of the nails and in His side the glorified scar of the sword thrust. It is the worship of the Father as He is revealed by the continuing humanity. And, secondly, it is to see the representation of that priesthood in the midst of the congregation. In the mystery, all our worship is round the altar in heaven: for we too are already dead. We too, the epistle to the Ephesians assures us, are even now at the right hand of God. Our citizenship is in heaven. We also are ascended " and with Him continually do dwell." But because our " embassage " is on earth we must represent here His constant and glorified sacrifice.

We do not follow the pattern of the last chapter where we sketched the actuality, and then sought to rise above it. Even cut off from the work of the congregation and from the obligations of personal devotion, our subject is vast. Selectiveness is demanded by the extent of the issues. The reader may be assisted by an immediate outline of the selection.

Two preliminary notes are required, concerning the mode and form of our worship, if later we are not to be misunderstood. Then under three short heads we will recall the nature of the High Priesthood. Finally its manifesting in His earthly ministry will call forth obligations that must be figured out in the worshipping life of the fellowship.

THE MODE AND FORM OF WORSHIP

All attempts at recovered forms of worship, in Scotland, are endangered by the prejudice that what is essayed is not " Presbyterian." It is therefore worth recording that Presbyterianism is a form of Church *government*. A review of " Presbyterian " worship during the last four centuries would be sufficient to remind us that it has never had a constant mode or form. When we are asked to " get back to the worship of our fathers " we are well entitled to ask, " Which of our fathers ? " For our worship has never stood constant. The introduction of the metrical psalms caused a flutter in their day : and no wonder, for many of them were written by an Englishman, the Provost of Eton. While, later, hundreds of folk deserted the churches when the paraphrases were introduced. Again, what is the " presbyterian form " of frequency in administering the sacrament of Holy Communion ? Is it John Calvin's plea for a return to the scriptural practice of a celebration each Lord's Day ? Or is it John Knox's practice in his acceptance of it once a month ? Is it that peculiar episode when the Church of Scotland upbraided the Church of England for their infrequency in celebration ? Or is it the period later still when the observance was once or twice a year ? To which of " our fathers " do they wish us to return ? Or, coming to our own day, is the norm constituted by those 1,300 of our churches where it is observed no more than twice a year, or by those where it is celebrated once a month, or by those where it is celebrated every Sunday, now in this present time ? If the vast majority, with bi-annual observance, represents the norm then are we true to Holy Scripture ?

There is no norm : nor am I hinting that the General Assembly should enjoin one. Increased frequency must march with increased awareness of what it is we do. Nor will the awareness be manifest till a congregation recalls to its consciousness the continuing High Priesthood of the Man in heaven. The true presbyterian is he who, in this and all things, is challenged by the promptings of the Holy Spirit as He speaks to our day, in the light of scripture. There is no constant " experience of the Church " to which to make appeal. The road is open.

Again, there is no " Presbyterian " approach to the Sabbath. With John Knox playing bowls on Sunday, the 18th century eschewing games completely, and our own hesitant fashioning— somewhere between—there is no norm. Indeed the issue is raised whether there ever should be : whether, for instance, right observance in the noisesome city and in the quiet country place should not always differ. At least in deciding let us be clear that Sabbatarianism was never a principle of our Church. Puritanism was once a principle of which Sabbatarianism was the Sunday expression. Puritanism scorned the muse of music and of beauty, destroyed the bagpipes and condemned the theatre. And the moment our people have accepted gaiety into the colour of their homes, secular music by the hour through the wireless, the theatre, on the screen and a Festival of the Arts, they have departed from the Puritan principle of life. For anyone to suggest that, in such an environment uncondemned, we should somehow retain its vestigial remainder in our witness on one day of the week is not loyalty to our fathers but a form of affectation. To whitewash what should be the most colourful day of the week, in a world of secular high colours, may well bedevil other and more important things that we have to say to youth.

Yet it is right to add that no church that drops its disciplines

99

can deepen its life. If the rigorous Sunday be dropped, we have an obligation to recover its purpose in the alternative technique that disciplines the wider Church, in the observance of the Christian year and the rigorous restraints of Lent. We must recover some pattern of restraint and for the rest feel free to fashion Sunday as will best portray for modern man the presence of the living God.

Secondly, to release us from subsequent misunderstanding, there is no Presbyterian form of conducting worship, or observing it. I have heard it often claimed that " Presbyterians " sit to pray. It is well to remember that for a long period they knelt and for a longer period they stood. It was less than a hundred years ago that Presbyterians first thought to be seated while in corporate prayer : having neither the church furniture that allowed of kneeling nor the old stamina that assisted them to stand. While the living God is gracious to hear us in whatever manner we approach Him, let us not be holden of fantastic notions. Again, and more importantly, John Knox said his creed each day at the daily service : and not infrequently read his prayers. Jenny Geddes threw her stool in St. Giles' not because the Dean was reading his prayers but because he read them from an unfamiliar book. (It is to be regretted that the instant that she chose is said to have been the moment that he was praying, " O God, who art the Author of peace and the Lover of concord " !)

It is true that in another period they counted it deadness to be anything but extempore. In our day we have the mixed tradition. Not infrequently it is to be feared we resort to what seems almost a dissembling before the Lord ; when ministers learn up by rote on Saturday a precise sequence of ironclad scriptural phrases that on Sunday they may appear unto men to be moved by every rustling of the Spirit.

There is indeed a problem here for many of our people, let alone the enquirer who comes in. As in so much else we are at the meeting of the tides. If formal liturgy was thesis, and extempore prayer was antithesis, a new synthesis must be found. It is significant that in the early Church the two were constantly blended but to elaborate its modern application would be disproportionate to the main purpose of this chapter. He was wise who said, " If all men could pray always as some men can pray sometimes, there would be no need of formed prayers." What must be done is, once more, to move fearlessly on an open road, culling from differing strands in our past such growths as will best adorn our time. " If I drink oblivion of a day, so shorten I the stature of my soul."

These two antecedent notes, concerning the mode and form of worship, are designed not only to lessen prejudice but to clear the way for more fundamental issues. Not the least of our problems in recovering adequate worship is that too constantly do we keep the issues to such comparatively minor points. They can never be solved till we are lifted to a higher conception of what it is in corporate worship that we do.

THE HIGH PRIESTHOOD OF CHRIST IN THE MIDST OF THE CONGREGATION

We have seen the pathos of modern man, not altogether unconscious of his former state, his lost power of prophecy, his defaced priesthood, his desire to reign gone rancid. All the constructions of his intellect, the strivings of his conscience, the efforts of his will are his glorious but vain attempts to recover the prophetic, priestly and sovereign rights that were his portion before the Fall.

Stated positively, only in communion together and in Christ will we see God's pattern as it really is and be truly prophetic. Only so will we recover our sovereign dominion over the natural world. That this may be accomplished we must recover our vision of the High Priest. Only by our identification, by grace, with this priesthood will our consciences be cleared and our wills enabled " to do exceedingly abundantly above all that we ask or think." Modern blinded man wants what we have to give. Centrally in Divine Worship we are exercised in the appropriation of this high priesthood.

By virtue of the glorious humanity in the heavens there are three cleansings made available; the cleansing and uplifting of our spirits, of our bodies, and of the earth.

THE CLEANSING OF OUR SPIRITS

It is still in the consciousness of our people that we come to church to appropriate forgiveness. But is this as dynamically conveyed as it might be ? In the splendid words of the Church of England Prayer Book, " He pardoneth and absolveth all them that do truly repent *and unfeignedly believe His Holy Gospel.*" Pardon comes not just from penitence but from active belief. If our people understand penitence do we dramatically enough and contemporaneously convey its consequence in the fruit of a new life ? They are entitled to feel empowered as well as abased. May the partial nature of the experience be because, as it were, we convey a promise rather than picture a release ? We offer the look-back at the transaction of the Cross rather than the up-look and up-lift that conveys a victory. What was effected by Christ was not merely a transaction to be recalled but a high priesthood for ever to be availed on. What out spiritual eyes are bidden to see is not just the Figure on the Cross but that Figure ascended, in His side the shadow of the glorified sword-thrust. He leads captivity captive: releasing us that we may be chained to Him. But do we adequately convey in addition that " He gives gifts to men " : the Holy Spirit: the gift of all good things to them that ask Him ? Or, in another figure, do we convey the intoxicating offer of St. Paul that not only is Christ at the right hand of God but that we with Him are there already ? We still pray " through Jesus Christ our Lord " : but is the proximity of this relationship apparent ? Is the fact that " with Him we are ascended and continually do dwell " part of our consciousness ?

Not only are we renewed in spirit by our penitence but empowerd by unfeignedly believing the whole Gospel. It is identification with Him as High Priest that assists us to see Him as King of the situation to which, from our worship, we return. If our consciences are really to be cleansed from dead works to serve the living God, we must portray a living High Priest and not just the memory, however central, of a transaction on the Cross.

As we have already quoted from Dr. Phillips' paraphrase of the Epistle to the Hebrews—" Let us not lay over and over again the foundation truths. Repentance from the deeds that lead to death . . . no : if God allows, let us go on."

It is the vision of the everlasting and thus present High Priest that allows us to go on.

THE CLEANSING OF OUR BODIES

But there is a second benefit of Christ's death to be appropriated in worship that is best conveyed in the figure of the High Priest. Contemporaneous with the regeneration of our spirits is the redemption of our bodies. In the days of His flesh, Christ had not only a reasonable soul but a human body : the whole nature of the seed of Abraham. It is His complete humanity which is ascended. In the torrential words of Edward Irving " He took our flesh and made it holy and thereby made us holy and therefore will make everyone holy who believes in Him. He came into our battle and trampled underfoot Satan, the world and the flesh : yea all enemies of living man. And was He not Holy ? Holy in His mother's womb. Holy in His childhood. Holy in His advancing. Holy in His maturity. Holy in His resurrection. Holy in His ascension. And not more Holy in one than in another."

He took our flesh and made it holy. We speak of the law of the flesh as at enmity with the law of the spirit. But we will not release men from the thrall of the flesh, if we offer men only a spiritual redemption. And our flesh is not only our animal natures and instincts. Our flesh is our heart, whence all evil thoughts do proceed. Also, according to St. Paul, the desire of our minds is in condemnation with the desire of our flesh. Our wills too are subject to vanity. Heart, mind and will, prisoners of our circumstances, are of the body. If we are to be delivered from dead works, we must have the promise of sanctification in the outer man as well as in the inward parts. It is this promise that is sealed in the resurrection of the body of our Lord to the heavenly place. Thus, in extension, St. Paul can speak of the bodies of the baptised as married into the Body of Christ by His Resurrection from the dead : and of our bodies washed with pure water. Indeed, unless there is this regeneration of bodies as well as spirits, how can our apostle dare command us to present our bodies a living sacrifice, as our reasonable service ? While this is theologically agreed by the reader, can we pretend there is adequately conveyed to our people this wholeness of salvation ? That there is a spiritual benefit is understood : but it is the heart that " mak's us richt or wrang " and how wrong are our hearts. It is the mind that must take into itself the assurance of forgiveness and how tainted are our minds.

Again, this partial failure is due to men's minds being carried back to a transaction once wrought instead of being carried up to the Eternal Transactor who in His glorified body now pleads our total sanctification in the heavenly place, by reason of that which was wrought. If men could be so persuaded they would indeed be empowered to " go on " and show forth the outlines of a victorious Church.

Before passing from this second aspect of our redemption made clear by the high priesthood let us, however inadequately, note that it is the body of the Church that is lifted up. To get on we have individualised the offer, which is indeed to each. But we must see ourselves as parts of One Body in the trans- action. The " priesthood of all believers " has come into new currency and is with justice used to elevate the laity into a sense of their priestliness. The carpenter's bench can truly be elevated into an altar and so on. But do not let us limit this new coinage only to be used as small change. The fulfilling of the individual truth is the all-embracing one that we together, all believers, are the royal priesthood, the peculiar people that belong to Him, caught up into the heavenly place. Not the small change but the "million dollar" offer is to be availed on by us all together and must be bodied forth in our worship.

THE CLEANSING OF THE EARTH

But there is a third benefit caught up in the heavenly priesthood of His glorious humanity. Of this we know little but it is urgent that we know more. It is the sanctification not only of our spirits and bodies but of the earth itself.

What is the case for this claim? For, as we shall see in the close of this chapter, it much concerns the practical issues of our day. Let us state it in modern terms. Each of us carries in his make-up a replica of the whole created order. Put absurdly, if anyone gets 'flu the medicine has a common taste. It is because there is *iron* in our constitution that requires re-inforcement. For other illnesses we get herbs. Nor will any deny that the animal is in each of us. Each of us is a walking replica of our universe, mineral, vegetable, animal. Now when Jesus took upon Himself our human flesh He was perfect Man, or perfectly a man. And by doing so He released the whole constitution of man from the dominion of death when He rose in a body from the grave. And, in man, he released the whole created order.

In Bible terms this thought is there in the earthly sacrifices which were " for a type." With the offering of the blood there was conjoined the fruits of the earth. Also, under the law, the first fruits of beasts and the first fruits of the ground were holy as were the first fruits of man. Melchizedek, type of the eternal priesthood, gave bread and wine to Abraham. The prophets, looking to the final peace, saw the wolf lying down with the lamb and in place of the briar saw coming up the fir tree. So Paul was holden of this thought when he foresaw that the creation itself would be delivered from the bondage of corruption into the liberty of the glory of the children of God. Both St. John and St. Peter took up the vision of a new heaven *and a new earth* where right relations would triumph and all would cry glory. It is the earnest of this that is already in our bodies, and in the Body of the Church on earth. Already we are, in prophecy, part of the restoration of all things. It is this that is constantly held before us by the vision of Christ the High Priest in the midst of all things : the present renewer of spirits, of bodies and of the earth.

SUMMARY

This great vision must control us both in our work, which becomes worship, and in our worship, which becomes a work.

In the next chapter, concerning the kingship of Christ, we shadow forth the *work* demanded of churchmen in the political sphere where "we do not see all things subject unto Him." The Christian's unique contribution there will be guided by his determination, none the less, " to see Jesus crowned with glory and with honour." Thus will he retain his vision of the High Priest. Politics become one area of his " diaconate " as he serves in the outercourts of the High Priest who is also his King. His conscience, cleansed of dead works, will enable him, " If God allows, to go on."

But to keep this vision clear we are called to see our worship as a work. The high priesthood will mean little if it is merely the subject of an occasional sermon. Christ's eternal action in heaven must be constantly bodied forth in responsive acts in that embassy which is every local congregation. These acts are to be found in the Sunday worship and in the priestly, as complementary to the prophetic, work of the congregation.

THE SUNDAY WORSHIP OF THE CONGREGATION

It is clear that the retention of the vision requires sacramental worship. This is not to introduce anything new to the true Presbyterian tradition. We have already noted that the Reformers sought to recover this emphasis by making, as in scripture, the sacrament the normal centre of worship on the Lord's Day. Baulked of a weekly celebration John Knox not only instituted it each month but designedly ordered morning worship (when the bread and wine were not in evidence) to represent a sacramental occasion.* Nor was the essence of this idea forgotten even when the Sacrament was most rarely distributed. The simplest form of presbyterian church in the " low days " of the eighteenth century still retained the double doors with, between them, the pulpit. This was designed that folk might go in at one door, be seated at the long table below the pulpit, and go out from the other door when the Word had been heard and the sacrament had been partaken. Presbyterian ministers are still ordained co-equally to the ministry of the Word and sacrament. Our priestly function is co-equal with our prophetic. The Word spoken and the action done, the very burden of the Hebrew tradition and the central intention of this book, cannot be dissociated. And while we must rightly retain the primitive custom of never celebrating without preaching, it is high time that we recover the other aspect of their mutual importance not as something novel but as traditional, scriptural and necessary. What preacher has not known his words empowered, either in administering baptism or in celebrating communion, when he can point to the living symbols as climax to his words ?

Only with a greater centrality for the two sacraments can we body forth again the consciousness of the High Priest in the midst. We are so exercised assuring our people that we have not an altar but a holy table of communion that we fail to convey to them that indeed we have an altar in heaven and a High Priest in constant offering and intercession. In fact only the constant of the heavenly altar can generate the majesty of our fellowship which the table of holy communion was, as a phrase, intended to emphasise. Short of a living sense of a High Priest in Heaven, our minds are cast back to a transaction of long ago. All stems indeed from that transaction but what inspires is the present and prevailing

---

*See Dr. W. D. Maxwell's *John Knox's Genevan Service Book*. See also suggested plan at the end of this chapter.

power of the Transactor now all glorious in heaven with, in His hands the marks of the nails and in His side the scar of the sword thrust.

THE SACRAMENT OF HOLY BAPTISM

From all that has been said, what in holy baptism will be recovered in the mind of the worshipper ? Firstly, he will be reminded that it is the whole child that is made new. Denied the proffering of total immersion how many parents get a vague impression of a superficial sprinkling by the Holy Spirit ? How few parents get the sense of awe that must accompany the truth that the whole humanity of the child is lifted into the total humanity of the Body of Christ. Infants have hardly highly developed consciences so our impoverished discussions doubt the significance of infant baptism. But infants have fully developed hearts and all the latent apparatus of mind. And it is the heart and mind that is made new. Only in a new heart and mind can consciences develop straight : constantly renewed though that conscience must be by the intercession of the High Priest. This, you say, gets rather " mechanistic." Of course it does unless we also make the second and conjoined recovery : that to be baptised " into Christ " means the entry of the child into the holy congregation which is His Body on earth. For the life of the fellowship is the life of Christ. The God revealed is the God concealed in the believing parents in the midst of the believing congregation. " Christ has no hands now but our hands " and no Body for our contacting but the body of the congregation. Thus it is not isolatedly the gift of the Holy Spirit that is conveyed in baptism. In the book of Acts Cornelius receives the Holy Spirit before baptism, the Samaritans receive it after baptism, while others receive it at baptism. At first sight this must seem confusing to anyone who attempts to be a " systematic theologian " ! But there is no confusion if we recall that baptism is primarily incorporation into a Body. In this connection, the way Scotland clings to good old practice is intriguing. While we have no official place for Godmothers it is still common practice for an unofficial person, some aunt or friend, to appear who " carries the child " to the font. This is a relic of the idea of sponsorship. Strictly, too, according to our standards, when the parents, and no sponsor, present the child they do so not in virtue of parenthood but in virtue of their membership in Christ. In either custom they are representative of the whole congregation whose obligation it is to ensure that nurture whereby there is " growth in grace," without which no act of baptism is fully valid. Herein is the safeguard against any mechanistic interpretation. It is literally true that the benefits of Christ cannot be appropriated except as they are bodied forth in the life of the Christian home and congregation. Thus, for the recovery that we seek, the sacrament of baptism must normally be performed in the sight of the whole congregation. Granted a living congregation a child can be converted at baptism. " Buried with Christ in baptism they rise with Christ to newness of life." When an old Scotch minister invariably prayed " grant that this child may be so truly baptised that he need never be converted " he was pleading no magic transaction but beseeching that the great High Priest who received the child at the heavenly altar might so continue to preside in the midst of the congregation that the child might proceed from glory to glory. " Grace is insidious," writes Peguy. " If it does not come from the right, it comes from the left : if it does not come from above, it comes from below."

Thus, in baptism, we must body forth our membership in Christ.

THE SACRAMENT OF HOLY COMMUNION

What recoveries must here be made, for our soul's health, within the limits of our purpose ? Clearly we must be selective but the first recovery must be the sense of a celebration not unrelated to what is conveyed by the word in its secular usage. A Presbyterian minister in New York, pleading recently with his Session for a celebration of holy communion on Christmas

Day, was denied it on the grounds that Christmas was a joyous festival while this sacrament was the record of a death! Once again that session of sincere men were held by the vision of a sacrifice once made rather than a sacrifice completed and forever being pleaded. "This do to remember Me" can as truly be translated "This do to call Me back." If, again to recall St. Paul, there is a marriage of our bodies to the Body of Christ, what other name can be devised than a celebration? Thus the celebration should be accompanied by every offering of colour, every sign of gladness and every oblation of praise. Our people come to love it even more when it is so conveyed.

Secondly, and by the same token, we must convey the sense that it is not just our spirits that are comforted but it is our bodies that are fed. We are renewed in His likeness who stands at the heavenly altar. Our humanity is lifted into His glorious humanity. Herewith must also be recovered that what is saved and renewed is not only the individual bodies of the faithful but the whole body of the congregation.

I shall not here inveigh, as you might expect, against the use of the individual cup. However much it is to be regretted, the use is widespread among us. At least let us make a virtuous use of the necessity by assuring that all partake of their individual cups at the same moment. Thus can be expressed the priesthood of all believers in the priesthood of Christ. Further, especially where there is the individual cup, let us recover the practice of a whole slice of bread, rather than diced particles, being served to each pew. Then each breaks bread to his neighbour. Each is a priest serving, and being served by, his neighbour, rich or poor, young or old, "good" or "bad," shepherd, wise man or devout. By these practices conjoined it is the whole congregation that is made to feel it makes the offering, in Christ, just as Christ's living presence is dependent on the faith of the body gathered.

It is cognate, and important here, that we do not lose the greatest glory of the Reformers' recovery of early practice. This was their insistence on the presence of the whole congregation. We must guard against recent borrowings from Anglicanism, at its nineteenth century worst, whereby we incline to small and quiet celebrations " after the main service is over." As if there was any conceivable " main service " to which a celebration of holy communion could be appended! It is dangerous practice to have a full service of Christmas praise, for instance, and then, after the Benediction is pronounced, to gather the few, without hymn or colour, to what is the central act of Christian worship. It is Rome itself, and Anglicanism, that is now striving to recover what till very recently we had never lost: the sense of " parish communion." The whole " Liturgical Movement " in the Roman Church is their laborious recovery of early Church practice, which the Reformers presented to us and which we have merely to conserve. Liturgy literally means " the work of the people " and in this sense we are a truly liturgical Church.

Cognate to this, again, let us conserve the Church architecture that was fashioned to reflect this truth. The Word and the Sacrament must continue to be conjoined in the *sight* of the people. What irony it is that we continue to " improve " our churches by building darkened chancels. Such is to remove the table of communion from the people, at the very moment when Roman and Anglican are closing their chancels, bringing the table down into the crossing, that the whole body of the people may gather round the feast to declare their corporate membership in Christ!

This is not to say we should be satisfied with a pulpit three times the size of the table. Far less is it to be content with a table so phalanxed with chairs for the choir that it becomes the receptacle for their gloves, purses and the torn sheet from " Solemn Melody " which the organist has handed up, from the half-sunk organ so reminiscent of a small swimming-pool begun but never finished.

What is required for our vision is an equal centrality for Word and Sacrament, at a dignified distance from the nearest pews that should encompass them on three sides. The elevation of the table, three steps above the pews, gives it an immediate significance. Choir and organ should be accommodated elsewhere. The true Catholic expression of our faith would thus be recovered : the presence of the High Priest of our salvation in the midst of the congregation : Eternal Word and Eternal Act conjoined.

THE SOCIAL SIGNIFICANCE OF THE SACRAMENT

We have sought to envisage some of the aids that will focus for our people the corporate nature of our faith. It is in some such setting, for the mind and for the eye, that the social aspect of our work in worship becomes apparent. To speak of the social significance of holy communion is no longer novel. But it is time we claimed it as the central significance. Indeed it is the feast of everlasting life, but " hereby do we know that we are passed from death unto life, *because we love the brethren.*" It is not true that any of us will be changed into His most glorious Body as an individual transaction. We can only fully be changed together into that most glorious Body of His humanity as we are concerned together with our neighbour, body and soul.

God was always, in Bible times, correcting His people's understanding of Him through the impact of history. Thus He corrects us still. The great community problem of our modern world is how to share bread. The only conflict in which a Christian can now take part, without confusion of face, is the war on want. Only Christians know fully the true motive for this. It is because we alone see Christ in the least of our brethren. Nor will there be victory in that war except in the Christian way. But we need not expect men to listen to our method until we begin to declare it in the congregation and are as responsible there for the economic welfare of our fellow members as for their spiritual welfare. Failure " to discern the Lord's body," scripture assures us, brings death. The phrase has had many devious interpretations in the history of the Church. Rightly it has been applied to our Church divisions : our complacent separations indeed kill the power of our witness to one Lord, one baptism and faith. Perhaps at its most impoverished, the phrase has been applied to the morsels of bread left over after a celebration in Church. Indifference as to the disposal of the tiniest crumb has been argued as an indifference worthy of damnation. But let us dare the real significance of the sacrament and the real danger of not discerning our Lord's Body by a figure of speech. What should you do with the consecrated bread left over if you have just celebrated in famine town, say as a chaplain in Korea or as a missionary in some Indian plain where the harvest has failed ? There is only one answer. Put butter on it and give it to the children. As they gulp it, gulp down your own sense of profanity in the certain confidence that you are discerning the body of our Lord. " I was anhungered and ye gave Me meat : inasmuch as ye do it to the least of these My brethren ye do it unto Me." In the children you discern the body of our Lord.

If we had but eyes to see we all live in famine town to-day, in our unified world. It is because we do not see the centrality of the social significance of the sacrament that many among our church members are " weak and sickly and not a few sleep." To discern the Lord's body means to be challenged by the total welfare of fellow members of Judah in all the world and, for that matter, to be challenged by the total welfare of His brethren in Israel, every man-jack of them : for whom we are God's interpreters, stewards of the mystery whereby alone all men can be fed. Thus are we to show forth the Lord's death till He comes. When He comes it will be to a city, in a new earth where dwell right relations. Till He comes the Church prefigures that day, practising for it. We are, in symbol as was Judah, the fig tree. Jesus cursed the fig tree because it was not bearing fruit—though it was not the time of fruit bearing. It is a most immoral story unless it means, as it does, that Judah exists to bear fruit before the natural time for doing so. We alone know what the war on want is about. We alone know the secret of shared bread. Yet the distance the

Church has to go before it recovers its full mission of holiness, which is healthiness, is evidenced from the incident already quoted where, for a meeting on war on want, from four hundred churches invited, sixty persons came, while from twenty trade union branches two hundred came.

The confusion is not that the trade unions discern the Lord's body. The confusion of face is that those churches did not. Nor is it their fault. By a fog of false spirituality we have clouded from them the vision of the High Priest of our total health.

THE MORNING SERVICE

Indication has already been given of the Reformers' artifice in making the morning service a replica of a sacramental occasion when the civil magistrates denied their desire for a weekly celebration. The suggested sequence at the end of this chapter explains well enough what can be done. Here only two notes are required. Where a congregation is of sufficient size it should not be too difficult to recover a frequent " sense of sacrament " at least. If there be already four cele- brations, it is not too difficult to carry the congregation in the additions of Christmas and Easter as occasions when holy communion should be central. On the months not covered by holy communion the sacrament of baptism could well be incorporated as occasions of similar significance. Thus a sacramental occasion can be recovered each month. On the other Sundays of each month the introduction of the offering at the correct place goes some way to give a similar centre to the act of worship. In the early Church the communicants were called " the offerers." And if the offering, in the con- sciousness of our people, be lifted above the idea of a comely disposal of our givings, or even above the idea of offering " all that we have " in His service, to the idea of offering also " all that we are," the sacramental nature of our worship can be declared *each Sunday*. The mutual prophetic and priestly obligation of assembling ourselves together will more clearly reveal to us the great High Priest of our humanity in the midst of the congregation.

TWO OTHER PRIESTLY FUNCTIONS OF THE CONGREGATION

Proper to this chapter there remain two further obligations. There is a priestly work to be done that might be called the extension of our corporate worship. We must, first, make available to our people the work of the High Priest for the individually burdened soul. This means the recovery of the confessional. And any abuse or misunderstanding that might arise from that short blunt sentence matters little in the light of the multitude of souls who are crippled before our eyes for the lack of it. It is still a surprise to most people to be told that nearly half the beds occupied in the hospitals of Britain on any one day of the year are occupied by mental cases. But there is a more terrible fact. At least half of them are there because of an overloaded sense of guilt. The head of one of our largest asylums recently recorded that he could release more than half his patients if anyone could assure them of their forgiveness. Taken together these figures appear to mean that at least a quarter of the people in our hospitals are there because we are somehow failing to declare to them the truth of forgiveness. Such is some measure of the urgency. But such is the pathological extreme. Tragic as it is there is matter for even greater pathos. It is the number of folk who will never see the inside of a mental home but who are living half lives because of an accumulated burden of sin. Indeed there are few of us who could not, when honest, record that too much of our own lives are spent in a semi-frustration and a greyness that ill accords with the freedom of the Gospel that we preach. We, with them, are too rarely aware that the burden stems from a failure really to close with the forgiveness of God.

There is, to me, a terrifying word in scripture. "Whosoever sins ye remit, they will be remitted: whosoever sins ye retain they will be retained." What terrifies is the latter clause. Yet we have largely made of the text a " talking point " about the techniques of the Roman Church. While we dally with our objective speculations, we are, by some omission, retaining sins in a multitude of souls. Hundreds are in hospital to-day, thousands are in greyness because we have not adequately presented to them in living present colours the great High Priest of our forgiveness. It is urgent. There is nothing novel in the Presbyterian Church having a technique of personal confession and forgiveness. We did not do away with oracular confession at the Reformation. We simply recovered, in place of what was then its bedraggled vestigial remainder, the Bible pattern of releasing souls. " If thy brother fail speak with him alone, if two fail to convince him, tell it to the Church, if that fail let him be anathema." Confession to the Kirk Session was the technique they evolved and, if dessicated in form, it continued into living memory. Now we have nought save criticism of Rome—and increasing hospitalisation and a gathering greyness for thousands of our people.

As in other aspects of this book I am not arguing for a return to past ways—I do not mean this *obligation* of confession any more than did the Celtic Church. I do not hint at a return to birettas and cassocks or the egoistic strutting of doubtful authority: such is not Scripture. Nor did the Session approach achieve the purpose. Nor, at the other extreme, would I be content with a vague recovery of " counselling." Such is already done well by a host of welfare workers. I mean the offering of forgiveness in the life of the congregation and by the mode of that life. I mean too its focusing—as also was done at the Reformation—in the hands of a minister or sometimes in the hands of an expert with peculiar gifts, be he clerical or lay, in the congregation. If Rome was thesis in this regard and our present unquiet is antithesis then synthesis must be found in ways that begin to become apparent but cannot here be expanded. What must urgently be recovered is the mediation of our High Priest, through instruments to be devised in the obedience of the redeemed community who are caught up in Him.

There is, secondly, another priestly function to be recovered by the congregation. It is our response to the action of the Man in heaven in the redemption of the earth.

One day there will be a new heaven and a new earth. We are they who know it and who also know the holiness of the very dust, through the action of the great High Priest. Thus we are they who must be exercised about the holiness of earth in the present dispensation. If hospitals are full by reason of our irresponsibility, there are fields all over the world, and recognisably in Scotland, that are becoming desert because we do not reverence the earth. There are increasing millions (our brothers in Christ) going to die of starvation because deserts grow where once the roses blossomed. There is soil-erosion through ignorance, and soil-erosion forced on men because of our colonial seizure of the better land, leaving insufficient land for native cultivation. Nor need we blame the settler, for when did he ever hear the Church assert that to exploit the land is to dishonour the garment of God, nay to do despite to the body that God deigned to take upon Himself? Country ministers must become concerned. Nor is it only country ministers. The issue is more minute than a handful of soil. It is the very atom itself, ultimate constituent of earth and of the bodies of men, that Christ has redeemed in the death and resurrection of His Body. Yet how do we intend to use this manifestation of the Body of God as it is found in the atom? Forty thousand million pounds *each year*, it has been calculated, is cumulatively being spent by the nations of the world in preparation for a war which scientists, atheists and Christians are agreed will settle nothing should it actually be provoked. There is no halting of this universally admitted madness till men recover their awareness of what it is that we manipulate for our mutual and conceivably common destruction. It is the garment of God.

The High Priest of our humanity is weeping in the heavenly place before the face of the divine majesty: still pleading the divine mercy for His children in this their ultimate rebellion. If we do not heed those tears, how soon will it be before we hear Him saying once more, " Weep not for Me: weep for yourselves and for your children " ?

SUGGESTION FOR GIVING SACRAMENTAL SIGNIFICANCE TO THE
SUNDAY MORNING SERVICE. (*See p.* 114)

Administration of the Sacrament of Holy Baptism (on first Sunday of any *month* which has not Holy Communion).	CELEBRATION OF HOLY COMMUNION (being the normative service of Christian Worship).	Each other Sunday morning in year when there is no Sacrament of Baptism or of Holy Communion (see John Knox Genevan Service Book).
The Little Entry.	The Little Entry. (Beadle bringing in the Bible).	The Little Entry.
Similar to Normative Service.	Adoration. Confession. Absolution. Supplication. ——— Old Testament. Hymn of the Holy Spirit. New Testament. Local Intercessions.	Similar to Normative Service.
Sermon.	Sermon.	Sermon.
Creed.	Creed.	Creed (or great Credal Hymn).
Offering.	Offering.	Offering.
Bring up the Offering.	The Great Entry. (Elders bringing in the Elements): to Psalm 24: St. George's, Edinburgh	Bring up the Offering.
PRAYER:— of Thanksgiving. of Consecration. of Offering. of Intercession.	PRAYER:— of Great Thanksgiving. of Consecration. of Offering. of Intercession. " O Lamb of God."	PRAYER:— of Thanksgiving. of Dedication " of all that we have and are." of Intercession.
The Lord's Prayer.	The Lord's Prayer.	The Lord's Prayer.
Administration of Baptism.	Distribution of the Elements.	Hymn of Objective Praise.
Short Thanksgiving and Thanksgiving for the Blessed Departed.	Short Thanksgiving and Thanksgiving for the Blessed Departed.	Thanksgiving for the Blessed Departed.
THE BENEDICTION.	THE BENEDICTION.	THE BENEDICTION.

118

NOTES : 1. While on paper this may seem too formalised, there is " significance " given to the sequence for each Sunday. Corporate worship becomes something that is " done." The morning service in our churches has a unified sequence anyway. This method gives meaning to its progression in the light of its sacramental significance.

2. Incidental sung praise has been omitted and can be placed where most convenient.

3. By a " great Credal Hymn " is meant the *Te Deum Laudamus*, or *St. Patrick's Breastplate*, or *Praise to the Holiest in the Height* or one suitable to the period of the Christian Year.

CHAPTER SEVEN

CHRIST AS KING
IN THE MIDST OF THE CONGREGATION

This chapter has been reset since its delivery as a lecture, due to the additional chapter that opens this book.

At the beginning of the last chapter, concerning the high priesthood of Christ, we warned that our response to Christ in worship could not be dissociated from our prophetic obligation. There is a similar conjunction needed between our representation of His high priesthood in worship and our obedience to Him as King.

That aspect of His priesthood which we noted last, His redemption of the earth, His cleansing of the atom, clearly cannot be made manifest, in His earthly embassy which is the local congregation, in worship alone. " Not everyone that saith unto me Lord Lord " (about our abuse of the atom), " shall enter the Kingdom but he that doeth the will of the Father " (about the atom). For this area of our obedience the figure changes to that of His kingship. It would be a happier world indeed if all that remained for churchmen was to decide what they were to do in this specific area of peace. Unfortunately there is a long way to go before the Church accepts that priority and it is not my intention directly to deal with it here. Not only, in our unified world, is peace indivisible. It is also true that you cannot divide the politics of peace from every other kind of politics. We therefore once more confine this chapter to the essentials that again must move our people if we are ultimately to be fitted for the greatest, most related, contribution that churchmen have to make in politics : the enthronement of Christ as the Prince of peace.

Enough has been said in our opening chapters to indicate specific areas where that obedience is required if there is to be hope of restoring a Christian West. We can therefore confine our words to some clarification first of the obligation of Christian political action; second, of the mode of its implementation in practice; and thirdly of what is presently required of us to manifest that justice among men which has been described as " love at a distance."

THE OBLIGATION OF CHRISTIAN POLITICAL ACTION

This can be summed in almost ejaculatory terms. There are few strict pietists about, and there is general agreement regarding our political obligation, but it is well to summarise whence the obligation stems.

The doctrine of Creation reminds us that the earth and its fullness is the Lord's. Therefore, for those who have been made new, who accept its redemption, it becomes sin wrongly to distribute the wealth of the earth.

The doctrine of Man in the image of God issues inevitably in the vision of each man, even the least, as having upon him, in potentiality, the image of Christ. This indeed is not only implied but explicit in His parable of the tests by which we shall be judged. Therefore, for those who have had their eyes so opened and who are committed to see as Christ sees, it becomes sin wherever political or economic injustice deface that image.

The doctrine of the Incarnation reminds us that in Christ is sanctified not just the spirits of men but their bodies and, as has been argued, the whole order of nature. " For well we know this weary soiled earth is yet His own by right of its new birth." Therefore for those of us who live in the perpetual light of Christmas, it is sin if we are indifferent to any situation that desecrates home or labour or if we use wrongly the stuff in which the Godhead freely chose to dwell that He might uplift it and present it unto Himself a pure offering.

The doctrine of the Atonement, as it completes the gracious work of incarnation, further reminds us that " all men are the brothers for whom Christ died." Therefore, for those of us who know our redemption, it is sin if we disregard the underprivileged, the guilty and the oppressed who, in Him, are also numbered with us.

THE MODE OF ITS IMPLEMENTATION IN PRACTICE

The above must suffice for the obligations of Christian political action. The sincere split among Christians resides in the method of manifesting these doctrines in the ongoing political situation as it challenges each succeeding age. Within the possibilities of our compass, we can confine the main difference between two schools of thought. We might call them the liberal and the orthodox. We shall attempt to summarise them, though later we must depart from each.

The liberal view which had a short if gallant life, coming to fullest flower in the nineteen twenties and thirties, might be summarised as a Quixotic charge at the Windmill of Sin. By-passing much that the Bible also had to say about man's condition, the limitations to progress in the world, the power of sin, and the fact of death, they put on what might be described as a verisimilitude of the whole armour of God. Inspired of such doctrines as we have summarised, they stood: having girded their loins with socialism, and having put on the breast-plate of right relations, and having shod their feet with pacifism, as the preparation of the gospel of peace. Thus they rode into the Windmill of Sin—to be unseated. They had forgotten, we might say, the sword of the Spirit which is the Word of God, concerned as it is with a depth of sin that they did not plumb, and the limitations to progress in the fact of death. But there was one accoutrement they wore which was no verisimilitude: the authentic helmet of faith. However disarrayed now lies the cohort of liberal theologians on the field of battle, they made a splendid advance from the crumbling ivy-covered walls of the Castle once correctly named Orthodoxy. They demolished all sorts of pockets of sin that for centuries had been allowed to fester within sight of orthodoxy. They left in permanent disarray any claim that colonialism could be an end in itself. They exploded the patronage that assumed that there was virtue in poverty—provided you were not poor yourself. They probably saved British socialism from becoming permanently dyed with the secularism that has bedevilled it on the continent, by giving hope to sweated labour that Christ cared for their plight. They certainly saved the working classes in the United States from the worst excesses of economic indifference that marked the turn into the present century. Had I lived their span I would rather have died with them, than sit at home in the Castle where not all but far too many were buying ever larger magnifying glasses to discover, by exegetical criticism, the effect of the aramaic on the original hebraic, as affected by the hellenistic meaning of the word charity: while German brothers were flogging natives to death in Africa and scores were dying of TB in the squalid acres of Pimlico. Perhaps the liberals partly built on stubble. Even so let us be sure they are saved: yet so as through fire. It is their faith that would save them. And in the measure of our departure from their faith we have suffered loss.

Whatever permanent commotion these liberal theologians failed to make in the world, they created a permanent commotion within the Castle of Orthodoxy. They forced a considerable number of the stay-at-homes to look up from their exegetical pre-occupation. They let loose a whole school of " neo-s." If the neo-orthodox are justified in pointing the shortcomings of the liberals, they should at least admit that they were stirred to life by their remarkable, if partial, victories.

To summarise the position of the neo-orthodox, within our compass, is a more daunting task. They claim a return to orthodoxy and certainly they recovered the full proportions of the faith in just such areas as we have noted the liberals let pass. That is, so far as the Bible outline is concerned. The trouble—that in practice too often causes them to be far less active politically and in that measure less Biblical than the shot-down liberals—is that in essence they pretend a similar authority for Bible *applications*. These applications stem in fact not from the Book but from the way in which the Reformers looked at the Book in terms of their understanding and of their environment. This too many of them do when the pith of our problem is that there is no sign of modern man, as we argued in our opening chapter, living in such an environment or such an understanding. For the Reformers the relation between the Church and the State was close-knit. Almost till living memory that relationship was assumed with a hundred strands running out into practice. It is, for instance, not far from living memory that our law declared a man could be tried in the civil (not the ecclesiastical) court for failing to see that his wife went to church! Again, it is within living memory that the Kirk Session was a court of the land: with public education and the administration of the Poor Law in the hands of the Church. Now while this was the consciousness of the people it was understandable and understood to make a division, for clarity of thought, between love and law. It is to this old division that the new orthodoxy seeks to recall us regardless of a new environment.

True to the Bible they do not dissociate piety from politics. They recover the Hebraic claim to their indissoluble conjunction. Thus one of their eloquent protagonists* writes:
" The act of faith which sets a man within the new community is an act of exultant solidarity, wholly spurious unless it issues in the feeding of the hungry and the clothing of the naked.

" What the New Testament faith does is to root the solidarity of mankind, as one redeemed Body, in the embodied love of God in Christ. The community of the justified men, in whom the circle of self is broken, is the community of those who, being ' righted ' with God, are set in a relation of joyous obligation with ' all the brethren for whom Christ died.' This new solidarity implements itself first within the koinonia— ' neither counted any man ought that he possessed to be his own '—but it shortly runs out into political concern and the care of the state, as soon as it becomes manifest that the com-

---

*The Renewal of Man: by Rev. Alexander Miller.   Doubleday and Co., New York.

munity of love must co-exist with the communities of law, and that the feeding of the hungry and the care of the poor is a political act. It is this co-existence of the community of love with the community of law, and the perception that the law of justice, like the law of God, can be an instrument of love, that sets the problem for Christian political thought."

Well said indeed. But where, with so many like-minded, he gets a little less exciting is when he neatly draws the explosion pin from such a bomb by declaring later, " Our prime necessity, if the community of love is to be fruitfully related to the communities of law (and Christian love itself to political duty), is that they be *rightly discriminated*." In expansion of this he argues, for instance, that " the Church has no parallel and few analogies among the communities of mankind. It is characteristic of the natural communities, the family, for example, that they both nurture and fracture human community. . . . Our Lord's ambivalent attitude to the family—His benediction upon it and His insistence that ' in the kingdom of heaven they neither marry nor are given in marriage '—is a reminder that even this most precious of human groupings is grounded in an exclusiveness which makes it provisional and far from absolute." Over against these human communities he further argues that " they have no equivalent in the Community of Faith. For the Church is constituted not by political *or any other kind of agreement*,* but by baptism and a simple confession of faith which represent the fact that what is being done in and through the Church is the re-establishment of the human community without restriction of political agreement, or temperamental affinity, or intellectual competence, or any kind of co-incidence whatsoever. The Church represents an undertaking paralleled nowhere else at all ; the taking of ordinary human material and making a family out of it."

That may well be a true description of the Church. I have quoted my friend in full, partly because it would be unsafe

---

* My italics.—G. F. M.

to paraphrase him and more so that the present reader may re-read, against this second description of the Church, the rather more exciting one which opened the quotations from his book. In all fraternity, he cannot rest in both descriptions of the Church. If it is the former then quite considerable things might happen. If it is the latter it appears to be about as soggy a mass as the world it came to save. If the Church is not constituted by " any kind of agreement," then it is as ambivalent as the human family, whose limitations he protests. It becomes inevitable that he later proceeds to say, " The characteristic political questions do not arise within the Christian community but in the human community. Political questions— concerning bread and freedom, education and sanitation—are human problems and not Christian problems : but just because they *are* human problems they are of endless and costly concern to Christian men. But as we work out our obligation in these typical political areas, there is no peculiar form of Christian duty, but only a peculiar Christian urgency to do our human duty well." It is in this speculative maelstrom that a flood of phrases bob up, such as that " Justice is ' the alloy of love ' giving to love ' the tensile strength to shift collective wrong ' " or that a Christian must deal with " Absolute loyalties and pragmatic politics. "

I can best clarify the dilemma in which this school seems to place us by a personal application. I, as a member of the Church —he seems to argue—have limitless insights by reason of my membership in Christ, but when I come to political decisions, which he calls the human area, I am no better than my neighbour. But am I really two people ? Too often indeed I am no better than my neighbour in political decision. But the measure of my inadequacy is surely the measure of my indiscipline in the service of Christ.

They appear to speak as if my absolute loyalty to Christ as High Priest can be secured while my obedience to Him as King can be pragmatic. Indeed when they relegate politics to what they call the human area I am forced to question what connotation is present to their minds when they hail Christ as " King of Kings and Lord of Lords." It is precisely this " discrimination " between the area of love and the area of law that unmans them for the fight. Thankful that at least they have lifted their eyes from the exact exegesis of the word charity, I must admit myself disappointed that most of them still sit in the Castle of Orthodoxy assured of His absolute priesthood within and hesitant of the application of His kingship without.

My criticism of the neo-orthodox, could I but expand it, would lie in these areas :—

(1) That they take over the Reformers' distinction between love and law and attempt to apply it in a political scene where there is no consciousness of law—as for the Reformers there was—as under the rule of God.

(2) That they imagine you can recover the Hebraic view of the world while in fact you bring to its criticism all the modes of Hellenistic speculation.

(3) That they forget the Reformers were inheritors of a view of the majesty of God which more accorded with an Eastern potentate than with Him whom Jesus Christ sufficiently declared by His witness of absolute love. They seem to side-step the truth that Christ revealed the fullness of the Godhead bodily. Christ declared " the fullness of the Godhead bodily."

We must not forget the terrible divorce that sprang up between the area of love and the area of law while " Orthodoxy " still ruled. We evidenced it (p. 71) in the remarks of Thomas Chalmers as he laid the foundation stone of New College. Nor must we forget that this was the dictum of the man who was the finest flower of social concern in the Scottish Church during that whole century.

The whole pattern of belief that erected Christendom, and that was manifestly of God's ordering for that period of His mysterious dispensing, has now got broken by the dictates of the same living God.

LAW AND LOVE

I know of no more telling presentation of where our neat divisions have led us, in attempting to " discriminate " our duty as Christians and our duty as citizens, than in a play produced not long ago on the London stage called " Captain Kavallos." The first act will suffice, for the description of a play can be tedious.

The scene is the house of an Evangelical pastor in the hills of Southern France occupied by the Germans during the Second World War. As a Christian he has a great reputation as a pastor. As a citizen he is leader of the local Resistance. Billeted in a bungalow of the pastor's garden lives, all unknowing, the district officer of the Gestapo. Being a local anniversary, the Resistance have ordered the pastor to kill the officer that night.

The self same evening the officer confides in the pastor, as a Christian, that he himself comes of a strict evangelical family in Germany: is its black sheep who, arrested by the superb devotion of the pastor, now wishes to be received in the Faith. He seeks audience of the pastor about his immortal soul and suggests a late hour that night. What, ponders the pastor, is his duty ? As a Christian he feels he cannot kill the officer in his unregenerate state : his soul would go to hell. As a citizen, if he disobeys the Resistance, he knows his own life will be required of him. He decides to postpone the shooting of the officer, now a Christian supplant. He will give the interview and put the man's soul at rest. Then perhaps next week, the officer by then fitted for heaven, the pastor may fulfil his duty as citizen and kill him !

The play is couched as a comedy ! " Ye maun laugh for ye daurna cry." But his family warn that he himself will be liquidated if he does not act resolutely as a citizen and at once. The pastor concocts a compromise. He will give the interview and, as proof of citizenship, will place a time bomb in the officer's bungalow to explode in empty air during the hour of their meeting. " But you have only a revolver," plead his family. " *No*," replies the pastor, " *I have any amount of*

gelignite behind the hymn books in the Sunday school cupboard.''
Down comes the curtain.

Such is the first act and it is sufficient for our purpose. Yet you may now want to know what happened! In a sentence, the play from that moment becomes unbridled modern farce: a turgid mass of mutual marital unfaithfulness among the inhabitants of the house. One would much like to know whether the author got tired of the awful poignancy of his play and simply transformed it into " good box office." Or whether, with terrifying insight, he was being serious all through and had conceived his play to raise the question, " If this is all the Church—at its most sincere—can in fact contribute to the greatest moral problem of our time, then why should we poor laymen seek to worry it all out? We might as well let all the lesser moral standards go too." Bankruptcy, the author is pleading, is all that is left for our indulgence in a world that has so neatly split its citizenship from its faith. Or, in the terminology of this book, we have skilfully mythologised the Man in Heaven lest we should have to reckon with Him as King of the Now.

For that story is not the story of a pastor in France. It is the story of the writer of this book and of any reader who admits the cap fits him too. Gelignite behind a hymn book is a much more comfortable crest than a Burning Bush. We have forgotten that " the place where we stand is holy ground." There is not " human " standing-ground where politics belong and some tabernacle beside it where God resides. There was once a Temple and within it a Holy of Holies. In that most secret place, opened but once a year for the high priest to enter behind the Veil and seek the nation's pardon, dwelt The Most High. When Jesus died, crowned with thorns, outside all that " holiness," the Veil of that Temple was rent from top to bottom. In Christ men saw the divine majesty face to face. He is High Priest of our salvation because from the moment of that revelation we know Him to be King. Wherever you stand now it is holy ground. *All problems are human problems—*

"bread and freedom, education and sanitation"—*and as such
are the immediate, and not just the mediate, concern of God as Christ
has revealed Him.*

It is from this stark confrontation that the neat divisions
of the neo-orthodox are too apt to release us.

Thus the Church, no longer challenged by the liberals, while
recovering the full proportions of the Faith, fails still to provide
that cutting edge which alone might cleave the growing secu-
larity of our world.

It is true we make our protests to the world in finer Biblical
shape than we used to do. But the world perceives our demands
on it are not absolute but relative. It was a do-gooder who asked
a hesitant labourer his wage. "75 cents an hour," he replied.
"You should demand a dollar an hour," asserted the do-gooder.
"But how do I get it?" asked the labourer. "Go to the boss
and say I want a dollar an hour *or else.*" "What do you want?"
roared the boss. "A dollar an hour or else . . ." "Or else
what?" asked the boss. "Or else," lisped the labourer,
"I will work for 75 cents an hour." It is not that the Church
does not make its political protests, and about the right issues,
it is that having made them, well . . . it can be calculated to
fall into line. In the days of four-wheel wagonettes it was the
fashion to have a spotted dog running behind, and even weaving
through the wheels, as the pair of horses spanked along. Sometimes when the conveyance turned down a wrong road that
could not lead them home, the spotted dog came out and barked,
but it was not long before it resumed its place, weaving between
the wheels. The destination was assured but the way to it was
relative. Our national state coaches take many wrong roads on
what should be the royal road to world-community. We
bark at the right places but the state coach-drivers know we
will soon come into line. Indeed the greatest criticism of the
Church to-day—and this goes for all of us—is that no one wants
to persecute us. The reason is a little frightening: there is
really nothing to persecute us about. No more than the man

in the street do we seem to have, in the serious issues of our day, the courage " to stand up and be counted."

THE MODE OF PRESENTLY IMPLEMENTING THE GOSPEL IN THE POLITICAL AREA

Having with an enforced brevity, which one trusts has not given the appearance of brusqueness, declared oneself alike dissatisfied with both liberal and neo-orthodox it remains an obligation to expose my own flank : no doubt for their brotherly cross-fire. This equally must carry the risk of ejaculatory statement.

Our perspective. It has been earlier argued that Christendom has had a great fall, and protested that it cannot be fruitfully re-created in an authoritarian way from above. (Such re-creation is indeed a possibility but it would be dependent on a failure of parliamentary democracy and therefore a reversion ill-attuned to God's purpose for our day.) The next stage of the world's rightful development is toward a world community that must be wrought out on the horizontal level by the suffrage of free men. We have claimed that this is what the Bible is about : a redeemed community. We have been at some care not to equate this with any liberal heresy that assumes a progressive and inevitable betterment, into a perfect day. It is enough, and it is certainly biblical, that at the last there will be a new heaven and a new earth, wherein dwell right relations. That this is a sheer gift of God and quite beyond man's contriving is not for a moment denied. (Equally our personal redemption, and for the matter of that, the next physical breath we breathe is beyond our contriving and a sheer gift of God.) But what is also clear is that God has created His Church as an early fruit of that redeemed community and has revealed to us all mankind as the children of His choice. " God willeth that all men should be saved." To requote my friend Lex Miller at his best, " What the New Testament faith does is to root the solidarity of mankind, as one redeemed Body, in the embodied love of God in Christ. The community of the justified men, in whom the circle of self is broken, is the community of those who, being ' righted ' with God, are set in a relation of joyous obligation with ' all the brethren for whom Christ died'.'' We do not know the time or method of the coming kingdom in its fullness. But we do know its nature, and that the condition of continuing in a state of salvation is that we practise for that kingdom now : that we act now, in Christ, as if there were neither bond nor free, Jew nor Greek, male nor female.

Our contemporary problem is that this corporate redemption challenges our time when no overarching authority can be re-convened, and when the sovereign claims of the nations in which we are set, and the exclusive claims of the national Churches in which we find ourselves involved, alike militate against rather than assist our vision of the redeemed community. The challenge also comes when, largely due to these distresses, religion has been individualised in a way that ill accords with biblical revelation. Again when, due to this further distress, our present congregations proffer a '' religious '' rather than a total salvation, this whole challenge of our corporate redemption strikes our time.

In such a perspective there is no other place to start than in the local congregation. Here must begin again from innumerable nodal points the nurture of a sense of man's wholeness and his solidarity with all mankind.

Our Marching Orders. These have been outlined in the social consequence of the doctrines that were summarised at the beginning of this chapter. But we could reinforce them with three inspirations.

(*a*) It is quite untrue to claim, as is sometimes done, that our Lord had nothing to do with politics. *The religious issues of His day were the vortex of the most explosive politics.* Israel was an annexed territory in a similar commotion as Norway might have been had the German Fascist State occupied it for some scores of years. The Sadducees were the collaborators, the Zealots were the resistance, and the Pharisees were those who, in all such scenes, walked delicately. The main body of the people were hard put to it to get bread. Pilate was the alien Governor, Herod the quisling. While Jesus came to speak of the eternal things, He did so as a Jew who knew that such cannot be dissociated from the historic situation in which God reveals Himself. Had His message been a " quietism " " away from all that," we would never have heard of Him, nor would the forces enumerated above. In fact He spoke to such effect, and acted so rigorously, about bread and forgiveness and kingship—speaking the eternal things in relation to that situation—that not one of those forces, from Pilate to the poor, could abide the sword of His tongue for more than two years. He knew nothing of the discriminations between theological verities and human needs. He was the At-one-ment. *That is why they crucified Him* !

The inspiration here is that, in any age, it is only in the real situation that the eternal verities come starkly alive : bread or forgiveness or kingship.

(b) Not only in Christ's life but in His explicit words there is the conjunction between our salvation and our social concern. It will be agreed that the very stuff of politics is bread and clothes and freedom. You can do nothing about distributing the first two commodities or conserving the last save by complex political means. These are the three factors that make or mar community. *And these are the factors that our Lord assures us determine our salvation* : *as to whether we do or do not feed the hungry, clothe the naked, and release men from bondage.* Indeed, most aptly for our time, it is the nations that come up for judgment : that nation is condemned now and to eternity that fails to meet the needs of the least of nations in their food, their housing and their freedom (Matthew 25).

The inspiration here, once again, is that you cannot separate salvation from social concern. Christ in His teaching knew nothing of the " discrimination " between the eternal verities and "human" needs. Indeed perhaps the most disturbing element in that parable is the explicit assurance that neither those saved nor those condemned had any conception that they were dealing with a religious issue at all: "Lord, when saw we *Thee* anhungered."

(c) In the early Church they gave to Jesus the title " King of Kings and Lord of Lords." It is a phrase that one associates perhaps with Handel's Messiah: or at least with that department of one's mind. One hazards the thought that if, at the next rendering of that work in the Carnegie Hall, New York, or the Albert Hall, London, the choir were to sing " King of Eisenhower, Lord of Bulganin," there would be a considerable exodus of people outraged that such mundane thoughts should be interpolated into so spiritual a work. It is therefore salutary to remember that this is what it did exactly sound like in the ears of those who first heard the Title declaimed. For it was as Emperor of The Roman Empire and Czar of the Assyrians that the phrase was understood and coined, to declare the significance of Christ. It was for such essential claims that the early Church was persecuted; so little was there a " discrimination " between the verities and the contemporary political scene.

OUR MODERN ENVIRONMENT IS NOT UNLIKE THAT OF THE EARLY CHURCH

As we considered under the head of " our perspective " the vastness of the challenge that faces us, and under " our marching orders " the unavoidable nature of our calling, we may quail before the demands. But there are aspects of our situation that are not unlike the experience of the early Church. If the days in which we live are sometimes called post-Christendom, they can also, and perhaps more fruitfully, be called pre-Christendom. We have their same tremendous message. Nothing is more moving than the exuberant certainties of St. Paul, as he lay with his sores festering in prison, when all that was apparent to the eyes of sight was the scattered little congregational groups—not many wise, not many noble— that then composed the entire Church. Similarly atomised are our congregations, as nodal points of freely-gathered men to recover the outline of the redeemed community on earth:

but what multitudes of them now exist in nearly every nation under heaven! Further, what victories of the Spirit, as we are allowed to scan the centuries behind us, support us which the early Church could only anticipate in faith! Again what technical assistances, summed in all our modern cliches of our now unified and interlaced world, present us, as it were, with a skeleton already constructed into which, by our obediences, God can breathe again His Spirit. If in innumerable congregations in unnumbered lands we can forge the outline of total communities again, committed to each other and seriously obligated to the world of men, it need not be decades before we might be permitted to see " What kings and priests have longed to see but have not seen." Yet the acid test will be whether we are committed to what the modern world calls politics as the medium through which the eternal verities come alive.

PRACTICAL CONSIDERATIONS

The first consideration, inherent in our case but which cannot too clearly be emphasised, is how fatal it would be if the churches in their conglomerate units, or their congregational manifestation, became allied to any one party. While parliamentary democracy still functions it is the essence of our health that individuals should work through the party of their choice remembering Her Majesty's Government and Her Majesty's Opposition as together responsible for the policies of. our land. The contribution of the redeemed Christian is to bring to bear his Christian insights both in his choice of party and in the ongoing policies that his party fashions. Apart from deeper considerations, any leaning toward a " Christian " party should be discounted : not only on the grounds of its sorry history on the continent but also because its success would denude the present parties of the salt they both welcome and require. Christians at present sincerely differ about the extent to which modern weapons of force can be used, about the priorities which will best achieve the next steps towards a world community, and about the domestic policies that will best lessen the dangers of war and soonest further our larger service of the world. *Their overriding contribution is the Christian insights they bring to the diverse solutions.*

Should ministers of the Gospel be involved ? Theoretically they should not. They should be so busy at the Holy Table of community, with all the duties that attend thereon, that men should see through them the Everlasting Figure at the Everlasting Altar, with perhaps, as Server beside Him, the African who carried His Cross. Ministers should be so interpreting the passion of Christ's humanity for all the dispossessed that Christ's tears communicate themselves to the very cheeks of the celebrant on earth, so that the laity are moved to go out and lift the contemporary cross from the shoulder of the earthly African. But this theory must wait on a renewed consciousness among our people that it is this kind of issue to which the redeemed community is committed. Till this total recovery is made, it is well for the minister to make open, if only symbolic, identification with the political obedience to which every Christian citizen is called. When in practice thieves enter a church to despoil the offertory box does the minister stand in his pulpit and cry " send for the laity " ? Or when a minister in his daily walk sees a member of his flock with alcoholic tendencies entering a public house, does he calculate which of his lay members lives nearest and proceed to a telephone booth that he may contact him to contact the man, lest his own reputation be defiled by following him into the public house ? These things are for a figure. Dishonest men are threatening democracy to-day and wandering Kikuyu are entering groves of bestiality. Neither will be stopped save by urgent political involvement. Woe on us if, at such a time, ministers confine our witness to sending for the laity. We can indeed endanger our hold on the absolutes by getting involved in the dirt of politics. To enter the body politic is always to be enmeshed in sin. But Christ Himself could only save us by taking our flesh upon Him, and with it taking our sin. There is one thing dirtier than politics: your heart and mine. But He only saves us by taking our sin upon Him. We may indeed endanger our reputations. But we should not forget that Scotland is peopled with a multitude of elderly men who lost not just their reputations but their jobs, their chance of pension, and full education for their children because they indulged in domestic politics when gross injustice was afoot. They are not in church to-day because of the delicacy of ministers' hands then. There is little such domestic injustice afoot to-day. But there is considerable injustice afoot among millions abroad who are our brothers in Christ and whose future lies in the decisions of our parliament. There are future Africans who will not come to church, nor should they, if we keep our hands white, fearing for our reputation when we should be involved.

We live in a day of crisis, and of such rapid evolution that future generations will reckon it more heavy with men's destinies than at the Reformation. In such a day did John Knox stand short of political involvement? As he stumped up the Canongate did he amiably remark to the passer-by, " Well, you know, there is so much good in both sides: I must get back to my exegesis for Sunday." Rather was his way, in a differing day, the way of safety for us. In such a day did the Covenanting clergy sit upon the fences of Drumclog or of Fenwick Moor? Had they not been involved neck and crop we might still be seeking our spiritual freedom. Is our only honouring of them, in a more urgent day, to be attendance at the annual open-air service of their commemoration, singing the psalms of David to the wrong tunes? To sit on modern fences is not even the best way to be safe. To sit on some modern fences is the quickest way to be electrocuted.

Even in the nineteenth century the ministry of the Church were openly aligned in party politics: the Establishment usually with the Tories and the Free Church with the Liberals. Whence then this *queasiness* with political alignment by the clergy as citizens to-day? It may be because we know upon our pulses that the issues are not so much political as economic. This is to raise issues that excite the blood. But it is precisely when the blood is up that we cannot fairly leave it all to the laity. Reconciliation is then at its most difficult. The ministry of reconciliation should at such a time know within themselves the pressures that are upon their people.

Ministers sometimes assert that the real political issues of our day are now too complex for their decision. If this is so they are equally impossible for the ploughman and busy doctor, the carpenter and roving sailor who also have the vote. If modern issues are too technical it raises the issue of the competency of Democracy as an instrument of Government. To succumb to this assertion is to rejoice the heart of the authoritarian who already lurks in the European scene expectant to take over. We must not succumb. The broad issues are clear enough.

I am of course not unaware of stories of some minister who has " emptied his church " by being involved in politics. But closer investigation usually makes clear that the dear man would have emptied his church anyway! Contrariwise, I know a minister who doubled his congregation in two years while not only being openly partisan in politics but also retaining most loyally on his Session his close, if argumentative, friend who actually was the local councillor of the opposite persuasion. That minister was not so foolish, nor should any of us be, as to use his pulpit for party propaganda. He was also perennially active in parish mission.

Having made clear the value, till the nexus has been established, of the open identification of ministers with political parties, even as were our immediate grandfathers, let us again emphasise a sane proportion in all things. The man forgets his primary vocation if his political activities lessen the efficiency of his pastorate or become the primary interest of his life. This goes, after all, equally for the doctor or the farmer. For the minister it should be sufficient if he does not hesitate to make his position known and undertakes sufficient witness as proves his position sincere. If a personal word may be allowed, I happen to have had a fairly pressured year and recently computed that I had given two hundred and thirty " religious " addresses in the twelve months. Over against that I have appeared on party political platforms on seven occasions in the whole course of my life. To judge by the rather intense correspondence I have sometimes received after doing so it would appear that these correspondents imagine I have given two hundred political speeches in the year and only some seven sermons in my life. (I have a sneaking admiration for " intense " correspondents. At least they are serious about the issues.)

Finally, within this clause, it should not go unrecorded that involvement here, similar to involvement in any real issue of life, opens directly evangelistic opportunities that might otherwise be missed. It is not long ago that I accepted an invitation to go to a rural village to speak to the local Labour party on the subject, " Why a Christian should be interested in politics." As the village was sixty miles distant, snow was on the ground, my car was of a pre-war vintage, and I had started late, I reflected for miles on the stupidity of my acceptance. There in the village hall, however, was gathered a hundred persons, mostly men. I could not conceive a similar stratum of the population gathering for the most advertised evangelical occasion. Not only was it a most fraternal gathering but I was asked back to speak on the subject, " Why politicians should be Christians " : probably the greatest evangelical opportunity offered me in that whole year. Incidentally, and as a by-product of the first occasion, the local minister while remaining personally friendly was politically so infuriated that he inaugurated, for the first time in history, a Unionist Association in the parish. This I counted a most salutary by-product. Thus are the eternal verities preserved and community life enriched when ministers remember that they are also men.

THE INVOLVEMENT OF THE CONGREGATION

The thesis of this book, and peculiarly of this chapter, if

successfully presented, should by now have made clear that to
"hitch on" political concern would be a wrong method of
approach. Political concern should grow inevitably from the
very nature of the Gospel preached and the Bible interpreted.
Evangelistic missions everywhere now stress that salvation
is for the whole man. When this is truly understood the
visitation to those in the parish is manifestly to the total person
who is called on. Where this is done the nature of the contact
inevitably leads on to issues whose final solution cannot be
divorced from social concern. In industrial parishes the state
of housing, the lack of playing fields, the incidence of tuber-
culosis, the economic plight of pensioners, Sunday work
(which unless it is faced will change the culture and religion
of Industrial Scotland in a decade), all lead us into political
issues. It is important not to pass them by as things incidental :
as if the spiritual were our department, comparable to the
insurance man, the gas-meter man, the health visitor, the
instalment collector and the rent-raiser in their departments.
So to pass by is merely to perpetuate the non-Biblical view of
religion already too present in the minds of our people. The
soul, in popular conception, is already a kind of canary cooped
in the cage of real life. The evangelist, in popular conception,
arrives with small portions of banana which he deftly endeavours
to pass through the bars of real life in the accidental hope of
contacting the mouth of the canary. Too often he leaves the
house unsatisfied, claiming the inhabitants irreligious. Actually
what they are interested in is real life and they are only too
aware that it is not summed in the whole gamut that runs
from insurance man to rent collector. But we do not get into
that life by peddling our brand to feed some isolated conception
called the soul. Christ came that we might have Life. Truth
is concealed in our whole environment. I do not blame the
boy who, from his experience in a certain Sunday school,
misquoted the text to read, "He came that we might have
life and have it *moribundantly*."

In the privileged parish, the ongoing conversation is of a

wider range and to meet it there is required a wider vision. Our Lord warned us in effect that visitation in such places would be more difficult. There are of course to be found there enthusiastic canary fanciers, who at least have the vocabulary from which deeper understandings can be advanced: and very often a disciplined spiritual life which secretly they feel revolves too much in a vacuum. The process there is long but is not complete till they perceive the spiritual message contained in those toy and gilded canaries in their tiny gilded cage that can be found at Woolworth's: their significance being that canary and cage are indissolubly welded. It is from these areas of relatively greater leisure and more privileged education that there should emerge those who, by their hold on the Christian verities, go deeper in their application of the urgent problems of our unified world.

In parishes, poor or privileged, it is well to remember our earlier discernment of the wise men, the shepherds and the devout in every congregation. There will be unreflective shepherds, practical men, who will become politically concerned by their service in the rehabilitation of houses. There will be the more reflective wise men who will find their place in the cut and thrust of political decision and action. There will be the devout whose prayers will burgeon with a more substantial content, remembering the nature of the final Kingdom for which we work and pray and practise, whose shape is a city and whose pattern is community. Here again, in corporate experience, evangelistic opportunities crowd in where the starting point may have seemed banal. The group in Partick who started cleaning out dustbins and lavatories were soon being demanded by the people to mend family feuds and stair-head vendettas. Indeed out of missionary China comes the story of the evangelists who laid aside their Bibles in a famine and concentrated on issuing rice to enormous queues of starving men. It was disturbing on the first day that about every seventh suppliant, his bowl filled, demanded of the servers that they should tell him about Jesus. Better organised the next day

they had a tent behind the open-air counter with the title
" Evangelist " pinned to its door flap. As the suppliants
began again to say, " Sir, we would see Jesus," the server
brightly pointed them to the Evangelist's tent. But without
exception the inquirers remonstrated, " We do not want
to hear about Him from the man in the tent but from you
who so costingly care."

Further, we have spoken already of the congregational
meeting and its emergent counterpart in the house meeting
where groups of the same congregation gather by streets.
We must not be slow to enlarge the interests of that street
by their correlation with the political considerations that so
often are part of the solution. In the parish meeting we must
go deeper than asking a candidate to speak on " The lighter
side of political life." Ask instead all candidates, national
and municipal, and not only at election time, to expound
their policies from a Christian point of view. From experience
it can be assured that they are delighted to come if only on the
dual ground that an audience is assured and quiet is achieved.

It is here we can counter the familiar charge that even if
all this were geared into action, there is little we can do, a
small minority in the land. We may be so. But a small minority
can go a considerable distance if it has clear objectives in an
environment where the vast majority just could not care less
about such issues. The majority are simply without objective.
It is said that, between general elections and not counting
paid agents, no more than two thousand folk in Glasgow attend
the policy meetings of the Conservatives, Liberals, Labour and
Communists *put together*. The national Church in that city
has six thousand office-bearers alone, before you start to count
the membership. Insist indeed on the prior importance of
the Church's work and keep two-thirds concerned with
ecclesiastical policies. But if, by reason of our crisis, we were
to " second," for the duties of caring for our world, the other
third, we could capture the parliamentary parties' policies in
a twelve-month by office-bearers alone : that is, from those

who might be calculated to have read the annual pleas of the General Assembly that churchmen should be in the forefront in the obligations of citizenship.

* * * *

In conclusion, three most general words.

1. We have been at such pains throughout to emphasise the indissoluble nexus between soul and body, between the preaching function and the serving, the minister and deacon, that we may have seemed to lean a little too far over to a mere mergence of responsibility. Of course there is a diversity of function. It is even an obligation in Scripture. In the Book of Acts they got in a mess as early as the sixth chapter about social concern in the matter of the Greek and Hebrew widows. To promote efficiency they appointed deacons to deal with such matters, in order that the Apostles might be free to continue " steadfast in prayer and in the ministry of the Word."

The first appointed as a deacon was Stephen : to look after the politics of the issue. It is intriguing, however, that within twelve verses Stephen, the deacon, proceeds to lift up his voice in the finest Christian *sermon* so far delivered in the ears of men. Thus early does the Living God remind us that if we are really to be loving we will not long be neat. " Would God that all the Lord's people were prophets "—and all the Lord's ministers were concerned with the total lives of people. The Word spoken and the Word expressed are the conjoined Living Word.

2. Again, because of our inevitable emphasis, it might appear that we advocate political concern in order to impress people or perhaps to come level with the Communists. This is not so. Benedict, in the last great upheaval of civilisation, drew groups closely around him not to affect the world but the better to recover the obligations of a total witness in obedience to His God. It was two hundred years later that historians began to claim that it was this single-minded obedience that in fact had saved civilisation. If Bulganin died the day you read these

lines, and western parliamentary democracy were introduced into Russia to-morrow, it would not change by one iota the urgency of our political obedience.

3. Thus perhaps our final marching orders come from the Epistle to the Hebrews. Nowhere is there better summed the nature of Christ's present kingship, particularly as the book relates His Kingship to His high priesthood. In that epistle we read, " We do not see all things subject unto Him but we do see Jesus crowned with glory and with honour." As yet, that is, it is only with the eyes of faith that we recognise His present sovereignty over all the world. With the eyes of sight we rather see with the writer of Proverbs that " all things are as they always have been " or, with a modern writer, we see " right forever on the scaffold, wrong for ever on the throne." Our marching orders are to act *presently* as if He reigns. We are the fig tree, whose fruits must be apparent before the natural time of fruit-bearing.

After all, we apply this principle to His prophecy and His priesthood. The hidden nature of His kingship is no different to the hidden nature of His prophecy or the hidden nature of His priesthood. Are we relative in our effort at obedience to His *prophetic* Word in the midst of the congregation or do we not strive with might and main to create His family now ? Are we relative to the offer of *His high priesthood*, saying you can't expect much of His forgiveness in the present dispensation ? Do we not rather plead with our people to be assured that though their sins be as scarlet they are now whiter than snow ? Should our response to His hidden *kingship* not be that now we should act, without a peradventure, as if the kingdom were amongst us ? There is no intended " liberalism " here. There is no promise that, if we so obey, miracles will happen in the outward sight of ordinary men. It is sufficient that it is the way of faith. To return to what Dr. Phillips calls suggestively, " The Letter to Jewish Christians " : the result of faithful response to His kingship now may well be that we seem to end by wandering in sheepskins and goatskins and living in holes in the earth. There is not much seeming social progress there. But it is worth recording that such is not the only reward of Faith. One becomes a little tired, in the light of scripture, with the " catacomb " school who gloomily insist that if the Church were obedient in the present crisis we would be forced into an underground. How do they know ? Another reward of faith, in that Letter, is that " some subdue kingdoms and stop the mouths of lions." We do not know God's design for His Church if it be outright in obedience. It might be that the power of the resurrection would be manifest to the subduing of kingdoms now in this present time and the wildest beast of our present problems become gagged.

It is certain that none of our problems will be solved by any other name.

There is a Man crowned in Heaven. His kingdom will one day be apparent on earth in a city. It will be a community and in its midst a Lamb as it had been slain. There will be no temple there for His temple will be composed of living stones.

It is for us to build a lovelier Africa and a lovelier Britain *now* in present faith of the coming King.

> " *O Lamb of God that takest away the sins* of the world,
> *Have mercy upon us.*
> *O Lamb of God that takest away the sins* of the world,
> *Grant us Thy Peace.*"

CHAPTER EIGHT

THE PRAYER LIFE OF A CHRISTIAN MINISTER IN A COMMITTED CHURCH

The thesis developed in these lectures implies a radical re-appraisal of the life of a modern congregation. In the development we have sought to wed high principle to pedestrian practice. As a scout officer in open warfare, during the First World War, I moved with the connecting file. Hourly I received, from the scouts ahead and the main body to the rear, messages of contradictory indignation. The scouts asserted we moved too slow: the Colonel that we moved too fast. If, by evening, these remonstrances were equal I assumed we were in the right place. In parallel, I have tried to keep my eye on the skyline catching an occasional glimpse of " the land that is very far off " while not forgetting the pace of the slowest soldier in our actual advance.

The skyline vision has been man's clamour for human community, whether evidenced in enthusiasm for the United Nations, excitement about nationalism, larger combines alike in trade unions or business amalgamation, in a very different sphere group-therapy in healing, or, at the lowest level, the enthusiasm of youth to dance in the largest ballroom and on Sundays to cycle in flocks rather than on tandems. This pandemonium of collectivism challenges the Church in its individualism.

But so challenged we find the Bible to be about the same thing in one sense and yet, in another sense, about a totally different thing. The transformation is effected by " the vision that is very far off." The Bible is all about community : from the Garden in Eden to the City at the end. From the ideal family that in Eden fell, through the reconstituted Israel, its apex in Judah, its fulfilment in Christ, its manifestation in Pentecost, its fellowship in the Acts, and its expectation of ultimate peace round the Lamb that once was slain, the Bible is all about community. The Bible takes man's natural search for community to remake it entirely. It does so through Christ who was slain before all worlds, manifest in history, and who, in St. Paul's inexpressible vision, when all things are subject unto Him, " shall Himself be subject unto God who put all things under Him that God may be all in all."

The Bible declares the failure of all lesser communities and the nature of this redeemed community by which all others will some day be encompassed or condemned.

This community is already secure for us in the person of Jesus Christ, the Man who intercedes before the Throne. The condition of our continuing security is that we retain alike the vision of ourselves already lifted up, our citizenship in Heaven, and the obligation to be His body on earth, His embassy in history. We are the germinating centre of His purpose. He is the Light of the world. We are the Light of the world.

It is to the recovery of this that our century is congenial. " The century of the common man " need not be a phrase of contempt, as if democracy were a grey thing. It need not be an impatient description of his materialism, because matter in itself, as the Bible reveals, is not contemptible. The transformation of common man into communal man, by revealing to him his eschatological dimension, becomes our task. Nor can we dissociate from that task the transformation of his body, the very fibre of his being, both personal and corporate. Else St. Paul could not have prayed that " our whole spirit, soul and body might be preserved entire without blame at the coming of our Lord Jesus Christ " : far less would he have asserted " Faithful is He that calleth you who will also do it." (1 Thes. 5 : 24). " For our citizenship is in heaven : from whence also we wait for a Saviour, the Lord Jesus Christ : who shall fashion anew the body of our humiliation, that it may be conformed to the body of His glory, according to the working whereby He is able even to subject all things unto Himself." (Phil. 3 : 20).

By the recovery of these fuller proportions of the Christian hope we face a re-appraisal of how persons are to be saved.

At least, of immortality, we know it is insufficient to visualise a series of individual souls, ascending a series of mythical ladders along the corridor of the centuries, to be received in a Heavenly court where a perpetual concert is in progress: the vague conception of heaven which modern man has so rightly decided to reject. Relatedly, much we have been taught about the pattern of everlasting life on earth, individual holiness, is transmuted by a return to the Bible. And it is the refiguring of this with which our final chapter is concerned.

Rather than confuse by speculating in generalities, the intention is to review the nature of the prayer-life attendant on our larger vision. For indeed a new personal holiness is required. In the same passage in the Revelation that records the final consummation there is the assurance that only the redeemed shall walk there. Into the final scene " there shall in no wise enter anything unclean or that maketh an abomination or a lie." Nothing written in this book must be construed as forgetful of our Lord's eternal word that " narrow is the gate and straight the way that leadeth unto Life and few there be that find it." Indeed a new puritanism is required. But it must be in the light of the community to be built: for which on earth we practise.

Let us dare a modern simile. In a recent film of mountaineering there was a superb shot with, in foreground, a narrow defile and leading from it a long " knife-edge " walk, a straitened way, with a sheer deadly drop to right side and to left. In the distance, in sunlight and eddying mist, rose a citadel of rock: obviously the summit for the climbers who were evident, like specks, roped together on the knife-edge ridge.

In the new way of holiness, that we have claimed throughout is the original way, what are the knife-edge decisions we must be making step by step ? Are they not all concerned with the nature of what is called " the material " ? It is Christ who, both by taking upon Him our material flesh to redeem it and at the same time denying its primacy, sets daily and hourly before us the challenge of the material, whether in the natural order or in the bodies of men. Here is the real problem of politics—when are they the passing passions of greed for power and when are they the only instrument whereby community can be built or practised ? Here, again, is the real problem of " Divine Healing "—when are bodies to be healed because they are the garment of God, which garment is holy, and when are bodies but the tissues of man's spirit, that spirit that can be purified by its victory over disease and death though the body remains unhealed ? The straight road of holiness, the knife-edge walk, is the daily, hourly decision, in just such issues. Confine the expansion of this thought to the political scene. On the one hand we have the command " Labour not for the meat that perisheth." It is the spirit that quickens, the flesh profits nothing. On the other hand we have the command to labour that men may be fed and housed and their bodies released from bondage. These dual demands force us into the ranks of politicians in their daily search for community and at the same time remove us utterly from what may be the motives of their search. It is the issue of heavenly and earthly bread, that alone is solved in the person of Jesus Christ, Son of God and Son of Man, incarnate and ascended. He is the Light of the world. But we are also the Light of the world. We are the Body of Christ and can never cease from the knife-edge walk of this obedience.

As we walk on this road of building community, we can slip into labouring for the meat that perisheth, not just in the politics of the nation or the town, but the politics of the home and even the internal politics of our individual make-ups—

> " When I invade my secret soul
> Seeking to find it clean and whole
> There peep at me from cave and den
> The ugly phantoms of half men."

Because the flesh profits nothing we are tempted to capitalise the spiritual, pass by the awful complexities of bread and houses and bondage—and, by our Lord's authority, we are damned. Or, because we have the insight that to care is noble, we can end by caring for ourselves, behind a false facade of public spirit, and down we fall the other side. It is good that we are roped: that we move as a team. Time and time again the fellowship restores us from temporary stumbles. It is merciful that our Shepherd is roped with us and in the lead. It is inspiring that, as Author and Finisher, He has been along this climb and knows its every foothold, has gone ahead to the Citadel and has returned to us " that where He is we too may be." It is as utterly abasing as it is exalting that once He "went it alone," that we need never now go it alone.

With Him we are " to walk in the old paths, where is the good way, and we shall find rest for our souls." As earlier we saw, the old paths were the way of social right relations. Yet the warning still stands: strait is the Gate, and narrow is the Way that leadeth unto life and few there be that find it.

Such is the challenge of holiness and the hope of holiness to those who accept the Incarnation.

TWO OBSTACLES TO HOLINESS ?

Two factors are apt to trip us up as we approach now the life of prayer. *The first frustration is that of loneliness.* So far are we from the Hebraic mood that we can hardly understand one of their proverbs—" When an Israelite prays all Israel prays." We must come not only to understand it but to make it our own. I often envy the techniques of Rome. One, to assist a sense of solidarity in prayer, is to remind their people that the Mass is celebrated every hour of the day and night. So far flung is their Church that dawn is breaking every hour and there and then the Offering is made. Christ is tabernacled with men, and with Him there is no distance of space or time. Thus each person anywhere can incorporate his seeming lonely act with the earthly tabernacling of our God on earth which, at that hour, is somewhere being celebrated. Bereft of such technique, it is healthy to remember that our loneliness is probably of recent date. Our immediate Presbyterian grandfathers rarely felt they prayed alone. Even if fortune took them to the colonies, conscious in their prayers was the little group then kneeling in the little cottage in the glen that they had left. A corporate commitment was the fibre of their prayer. But we are isolated now. In such a mood we do well to remember the constant intercession in the heavenly place and, in our offering, to feel identified with Him and with all who in Him dwell. But, if that be too demanding on our imagining, it is good, if only as a crutch for our frailty, to lean on some small committed group that daily pray for us as we do for them. The sense of membership in an intimate group before the throne makes less demanding the vision of the Intercessor in the midst.

A greater difficulty is our difference from medieval man: when so many of our " aids to prayer " stem from a medieval pattern. I have what I call " bankrupt corner " in my library and I am, if negatively, encouraged to discover it on the manse shelves of most ministers who have tried to pray. It is a platoon of bantam booklets enlisted at intervals to help one to pray better: purchased, as each severally went dead on us, on the principle that " Hope springs eternal." Why do they go dead on us ? Because most of them are written in terms of a different consciousness. Because most of them are conceived in medieval terms, we are not really conditioned to read what they are really saying. For medieval man life was dull, brutish and short. Life here was over against the real life of the Spirit. Indeed the Greek conception of the Spirit dominated their thought-forms as Thomas Aquinas was dominated by Aristotle. For the Greek, as we have seen, the Spirit was over against the body, while for the Hebrew the residence of the Spirit was in the blood.

We moderns are of a different expectancy to medieval man. Life is not brutish or short. We are girt about with possibilities. If medieval man looked up through a telescope, we rather look down through a microscope. Matter is so marvellous. If his fears were ghosts in the heavenlies, ours are in the infinitesimal but infernal and paradoxically infinite possibilities of hydrogen. One hundred and fifty years ago the only meaning of the word service was related to Divine Service. To-day the word conjures first into our minds the transport or the health or even the armed services. Again, in living memory the Royal Infirmary was two conjoined mansion houses looking down on Glasgow Cathedral, whose spacious structure could have contained them both six times over. To-day the same infirmary, nine stories high and covering acres, could contain six complete replicas of the cathedral. Modern man is earthed; materially environed. His devotions are transmuted. There is no advance in all this. We are enmeshed in this materialism. But the secret of our exit is of vast importance. " Back to devotionalism " would be as fatal as if our agricultural community went " back to the land " by selling their tractors and yoking bullocks to the plough. As it must be forward to the land, so it must be forward to the new devotionalism : or rather, as this book has pleaded in so many areas, to the recovery of primitive holiness. The key is in a serious re-view of the challenge of the Incarnation.

We have referred earlier to the " spiritualising " of the Faith that took place after Constantine in the third century. When the Church got enmeshed in a pagan state, the best among the Christians fled from so much materialism. Unfortunately they left that frying-pan to land in the fire. They went to the deserts of Egypt and met the streams of mysticism that rooted from the Eastern faiths with their denial of the body. And from that contact grew up a form of mysticism alien to the incarnation faith, which none the less, like ivy, battened on the pristine oak, and still enmeshes our ideas of holiness. They introduced the Via Negativa : the way of interior denial. Unfortunately the Via Negativa cuts dead across the Emmaus Road.

It is in this uneasy situation—(one can only rushingly indicate a trend)—that we come, from these little books, to suppose that the prayer-life is a series of rarefied spiritual exercises, if by any means we can attain. We must, they say, go through what the mystics called the purgative experience, forcing from our minds what is unclean. We must then be open to the illuminative experience, lest seven devils enter in to the heart made clean. Finally, if we practise long enough we may be granted the unitive experience when in a self-less stillness we know ourselves in the Presence. They are daunting instructions: Laboriously followed, we have known them to lead to what seemed like an achievement when, usually, on turning the next stage in expectation the instructor warns us that what we feel we have experienced is almost certainly bogus!

That such experiences, in more disciplined obedience, have some validity it would be blasphemous to deny. But I am convinced that few have the psychic capacity for such flights. I dare the further claim that such excursions are not even the royal road to holiness within the Christian dispensation, though we may be sure they are paths accepted by the Father of our Lord.

Yet how many earthbound mortals have departed almost completely from a serious prayer-life because they thought such the essence of prayer, and are benumbed by their failure to attain. Again, and it is here I question it as the royal road, how many who genuinely attain in fact keep on that knife-edge of practical obligation that is the urgent need of our time? So delectable, if demanding, is the exercise that they are apt to cut off the telephone when a whole world is trying to get through to them in the extremity of our need. None the less, it is these whom we are inclined to suppose are the truly religious, or the really spiritual.

Alternatively, the rest of us, feeling we are not made for it, embrace the practical and slither on to the knife-edge walk without sufficient prayer. We dismiss the bantam platoon, so constant now is the telephone. We comparably degenerate just at the moment when, if we seriously recovered the pristine holiness, we might have the word for our world.

There remain the cross-benchers who become hardly dependable for either school. Now practical, now spiritual, their telephone just ceases to ring. Neither to conduct a retreat or lead a " war on want " are they fitted.

We are immersed in the here and now. We know we must be. But too often when we turn to prayer, the isolation intensifies, the medieval resurrects and neither life becomes powerful nor prayer real. Such is the problem in personal terms. The reader will note we are each a reflection of our scene. As of the microcosm so of the macrocosm, we are a replica of our society; where the oratories are too empty of life and the laboratories too filled with the potentialities of death.

THE NEW APPROACH TO PRAYER

The key perhaps is this : if we are to come level with the modern demands of the Incarnation, we must take more seriously the full offer that resides in the Doctrine. *Personally consumed of the here and now we must recover the sense of God as Here and Now.

GOD IS HERE

This is to recall the evangelical offer over the medieval. It is to short-circuit the laborious stages of the purgative, the illuminative and the unitive: or, as we shall later see, to invert them.

But first of all it is to knock away again the props from the Scala Sancta : that stair of so sincere but fruitless an approach which Martin Luther grasped a saw to sever.

There are two straight ways of getting from your house to the garden gate. One is to proceed directly. There is at least in theory an alternate straight approach: it is to leave by the back door and encircle the world. Apart from the probability that you will meet with so many enticing attractions on the road that you will never get home, it is a faithless way. It is the

*As stated in the Foreword, for much of what follows in the thought, illustrations and sometimes the phrasing of the next four pages, I am indebted to *Behold the Spirit* by A. W. Watts.

way of noble works : and in prayer has parallel in the purgative, through the illuminative, to the unitive gate. But the lesson of the Incarnation is that you cannot do a thing about getting nearer God. Here is the Evangel—when Israel were dead beat and weary, trying with the noblest methods yet devised to get nearer God, in the superb words of an ancient prayer of the Nativity " While all things were in quiet silence, and that night was in the midst of her swift course, Thine Almighty Word leaped down out of Thy Royal Throne : Hallelujah ! "

That is the symbol, sealed in Bethlehem, of what happens whenever you or I want it to happen. If we being evil know how to give good to our children, how much more will the Heavenly Father give the Holy Spirit to them that ask Him ? We do not have to climb to God, or circle the world, with intellectual flight or devotional excursion. He comes down and He comes in.

Nearer indeed than even the garden gate : " Closer is He than breathing, nearer than hands and feet." We have been given union with God, whether we like it or not, want it or not, know it or not. Our flesh is His flesh and we cannot jump out of our skins. This is not pantheism. It is not a necessary or inherent fact of our being. It is a free, spontaneous and unnecessary gift of eternal life by the living and loving God. It happened for everyone. He took on the flesh of the whole world. God willeth that all men should be saved. Our only problem is whether we are going to accept it, be bathed in it. All we need do is to receive Him : and " as many as receive Him, to them He gives the power to be of the same nature with God." " The glory Thou hast given Me," declares Jesus in His prayer at the Last Supper, " I have given them." This was the joy of the early Church that enabled St. Paul to cry, " I pray that God will give you spiritual wisdom to know more of Him ; that you may receive that inner illumination of the spirit which makes you realise how marvellous is the power that is available to us who believe in God." The illumination is not a candle put in our hearts to penetrate only the most proximate gloom. It is an incarnation. It is bodily: the whole of us.

God loves the material element He has created and finds it in no way inconsistent with His spiritual dignity to stoop down and to unite Himself with the earth: with flesh and blood.

Here is the incarnational offer for us to avail on, if we are not to be broken by the vastness of the incarnational demand. Here also is the validation of our bodily and social concern.

This was the joy of the early Church. " We become Christ's member and Christ becomes our members," asserts St. Simeon, one of the early Fathers, " Unworthy though I be, my hand and my foot are Christ. I move my hand and my hand is wholly Christ, for God's divinity is united inseparably with me. I move my foot and lo, it glows like God Himself." St. John of Damascus, another early Father, states it in more philosophic terms, " We hold that to the whole of human nature the whole essence of the Godhead was united. . . . He in His fullness took upon Himself me in my fullness, and was united ' whole to whole ' that He might in His grace bestow salvation on the whole man."

How marvellous is the power available to us who believe in God! Call these extreme quotations if you wish, place them on the far outreach of orthodoxy as you will, but you cannot claim them unorthodox. What a necessary correction they are to the distance that is our prevailing atmosphere.

Here is the substantial offer to meet our so substantially material modern day. How marvellous is the power available to those who believe in God! God is Here.

GOD IS NOW

It is as necessary to recover our sense of God as Now. This in turn may sound so obvious that we must give it the content we intend. If, for the medievalist, God was " There," to be aspired to: He was also " Then," someday to be arrived at. Thus, for him, the monk was the type of full holiness. This was conveyed in symbol in the decoration of monasteries.

By his permanent vows of enclosure he was already in the heavenly place : thus the carving in the choir and sanctuary of the abbeys concerned angels and heavenly scenes. The carvings on the screen, the partition that enclosed sanctuary and choir and faced the laity in the nave, were classically of Christ's life on earth. So to say, only the utterly committed were in heaven, the rest had to think of heaven as somewhere " there " in the future.

But it is of the essence of the evangelistic offer that there are no longer two ways about it. Once more the modern Christian, if he is to deal with the burden of the now, must accept the offer of God's Now : His presence in the world.

For how, in fact, do you come into the presence of God ? God is spirit, no man has seen Him at any time. God is love. Love is never static but outflowing. So you do not enter the presence of God by seeking to achieve it in a pause. He is Reality, Love, Life and you cannot touch life. You can touch expressions of life, but you cannot grasp God who is the Life of life. Indeed you can only define how not to get in touch with life.

To take a natural analogy, there is a living flower. You want to have it, so you pluck it. But, by your act of plucking, it dies. You are fascinated by a sparkling running stream, a living stream of water. But, if you grasp it, it runs through your fingers. If you scoop it into a pail, you no longer have life but just a bucket of H_2O. There is a sunbeam dancing in your room, life from the sun. If you pull down the curtain to capture the beam it is gone. There is a bracing wind that enlivens your whole being. But try to catch it in a bag and you have stagnant air. All this reminds us how not to get into touch with life.

Here is the root trouble of our lives. We all love life but the moment we try to hold it we miss it. The fact that things change and move and flow is their life. Try to make them static and you die of worry. This is just as true of God who is the Life of life. The only way to achieve a sense of God's presence is to put yourself in the way of Him. In our analogy, you achieve a sense of life, in the presence of a flower, by a running stream, in a bracing wind, with sunbeams falling on the stream. You come home to say you have had a perfectly lovely day, which means a lively day. It has been a benediction of a day.

You can only achieve a sense of God in a similar way. Whether in the life of nature, or heightened in His life in men, you can only touch God in His cathedral of nature and of men in their unending flux.

You can only find God in the now.

There is a very attractive group of Buddhists who point this truth. The Zen Buddhists have monasteries precisely designed for busy laymen to visit that they may find God again. Such as come have been known to grow impatient with the subtlety of the monks' instruction. Here are some snatches of the conversation.

Business Man : '' Ever since I came I have had no instruction in the meaning of reality.''

Monk : '' Ever since you came I have been instructing you.''

B.M. : '' In what way ? ''

M. : '' When you brought tea, did I not accept it ? When you served me food did I not eat it ? When you made bows to me did I not return them ? When did I ever neglect to give you instruction ? '' Seeing the visitor did not yet understand the monk added, '' If you want to see, see directly into it. If you try to think about it, it is altogether missed.''

'' What is reality ? '' asked another business man. '' Walk on,'' replied the monk. '' What is realisation ? '' the man persisted. '' Your everyday thoughts,'' replied the monk. '' What is the one ultimate word of truth ? '' was the next endeavour. '' Yes,'' said the monk. The business man in growing desperation shouted his repetition. '' I am not deaf,'' said the monk.

B.M. : '' What are the characteristics of your school ? ''

M. : '' A table, a tray, a chair, a fireplace and a window.''

B.M. : " What is the religious life ? "

M. : " In early morning, how do you do : at night, good night."

The accumulation of such replies are fascinating in their assertion that God is now, as life is now, or not at all.

Of course we go further. God is spirit and no man hath seen Him at any time, but the Son, Christ Jesus, has declared Him. In Jesus Christ we know what life is about. We are to walk on to a goal we know. Our everyday thoughts are what He came to change. This He does among the chairs and windows, trays and tables that are our school of life, and in the innumerable contacts that form our " nows." The one ultimate word of truth is Yes : in Him is Yea. God has visited and redeemed His people. But the place of His presence is not in the then but in the now.

This strand has always been present in Christian mysticism. It is there in Brother Lawrence. It is implicit in George Macdonald, whose poem is in our hymn book.

> " I hear Thy voice, I feel Thy wind,
>   The world it is Thy word,
> Whatever wakes my heart and mind,
>   Thy presence is, my Lord."

It is its primacy in Christian mysticism that we must recover, as starting point in the new holiness. When in the morning we get to our desk . . . that list of meetings, the whole design of the day's life as it builds up from this or that telephone call, the man we like whom we are to meet at four, the man more difficult to like who will come at five . . . such is the bren gun rapidity of our warfare. How apt we are to wonder where God comes in ! Get through the grey, we are apt to say, and then perhaps at nine o'clock to-night, or nearer perhaps to eleven, we can have our time with God ! But " Whatever wakes my heart and mind, Thy presence is, my Lord." The great contribution of the Hebrew to religion, let us recall, is that he did away with it. Our innumerable and pedestrian " nows " are our points of contact with God in the highest, the apex of whose majesty is in His most glorious humanity.

TWO COMMENTS

Two comments may be arising in your mind, if you have got thus far. You may be asking, " Is the author hinting that there need be no prayer time at all ? Is he suggesting that life is sufficient prayer ? " I am not. In previous chapters I have sought to construct the body of the Gospel in which alone the heart of the Gospel can adequately function. I have sought to convey the kind of community in which God is interested. Such is the area in which alone we can fully hear Him speak. So, in this chapter, I have sought to convey the area in which true Christian prayer can take place. What debilitates our prayer life, I suggest, is our presupposition that the pressures of life are on one side while God is on some other side : interested and concerned but on some other side. With this supposition, when evening comes with an ending to our pressures, we are apt to go eagerly to God—disconcertingly to find a vacuum. We seek to fill the vacuum with " spiritual thoughts." The more we try the more desperate does the situation become : till in effect we say that we are not really the praying type. Thus we begin to lean perilously to one side of the knife-edge.

There are, of course, evenings when our prayer-life is refreshing : but, analysed, they turn out to be the times when the pressures have been so weighty that you have simply had to go with them to God. But this precisely is the recovery of the knife-edge. The religious moment flowers from the practical. Of the prayer life, too, we can come to say, " Hereby know we that we are passed from death unto life, *because we love the brethren.*"

The other comment that may arise for you is a confusion. " The author is getting at something," you may be saying, " But just when I think I understand I lose contact again." Well the author has no doubt that, through an abler pen, the moments of lucidity would be longer and those of bemusement shorter.

But I would also hazard that, with the ablest pen, you would find that you were missing and hitting it: with momentarily clear views followed by eddying mist. Such is the nature of our Citadel. For the mystery of true life is the mystery of the Word made flesh. In the true life of prayer we are forever on the knife-edge. We move in the light and shadow of Him who is born Son of God and Son of Man. Manifestly, there is a new prayer-life demanded: not stationary times with God, but living flowing times when, by His Spirit, we are exercised in unravelling the mystery of that apex of majesty which is His humanity.

It was said of a great politician that he rose at six to plot his day: not just to marshall his diary but to make his own the documents that would enlighten the flux of interview and telephone that interlaced his life. A well-known publisher, after reading his morning mail, endeavours to lock his door for half an hour and resolutely to face the particular issues that are likely to go wrong, instead of, like so many of us, skipping the difficult engagements that we know loom up and hoping for the best till the awkward—and unprepared for—moment arrives. Such again are for a figure. Both these men attained an altitude in advance that carried them serenely through their day. Such again is for a figure. Whatever wakes our heart and mind each day is going to be the presence of the Lord.

MORNING DEVOTIONS

Thus, in the morning, we resolutely count out the paper money of our plotted day till we have assessed its value in the coinage of the eternal. In the light of the Incarnation nothing is secular. But unless we handle each paper token of the seeming secular and hold it till we see its true value in the light of the glorified humanity then, by ten of the morning, we are down one precipice of the knife-edge and are in a like judgment with the pietist who has gone down the other side.

You may rest assured that all the old disciplines of prayer

come into play. It is true that we start with the unitive. We start with the acceptance of the marvellous offer of the Incarnation. But do you suppose, as we make our own such attendant thoughts as are proffered by St. John of Damascus, that they do not lead us into Adoration and thereafter to utter self-abasement and confusion of face ? The purgative necessity, of throwing this out from our consciousness and that from our characters, is every whit as demanding as in the older discipline. But it is no longer a disrelated spiritual exercise towards an experience. It stems from our experience. When we have wrestled with our state and given it to Him, the illuminative becomes our urgent need and not our pious obligation. In such a mood, the Bible is not something that " ought " to be read but its opening becomes a sheer necessity of our condition.

As the day proceeds and its engagements excite us, abase, exalt, appal us, arrows of ejaculation soar up, whose feathers were adjusted earlier as we prepared for our warfare and resolutely visualised the targets that the day would bring.

EVENING DEVOTIONS

When evening comes, and solemn assembly with our Lord is hard to rise to, we can go backward over the day and from this occurrence or from that it is not difficult to find reason for our thanksgiving or intercession and all too easy to recall failures that demand our penitence. It may well end with supplication that much of what became so secular to-day may to-morrow be transmuted a little closer to the sacramental.

THE VERY DEVIL

Finally, despite all, the devil will probably still get hold of us. We may find ourselves saying, " I thank God I am not as these pietists."

" In addition to my parish visiting, I have dealt with a criminal who has ill repaid me. I have been to a United Nations meeting. I have tried to share a wider vision with a trades-union official.

Indeed I have been involved. I thank God I am not as one of these pietists."

The devil will have got us once again. But of God's grace we will take the Book for a final illuminative moment. It will open at the story of a certain publican who went up to the Temple to pray.

Thus we will go to sleep in the mood in which we should always go to sleep: saying with truth, " God be merciful to me a sinner," and yet saying it with hope, for there is a Man in Heaven.

THE IONA COMMUNITY IS:

- An ecumenical movement of men and women from different walks of life and different traditions in the Christian church
- Committed to the gospel of Jesus Christ, and to following where that leads, even into the unknown
- Engaged together, and with people of goodwill across the world, in acting, reflecting and praying for justice, peace and the integrity of creation
- Convinced that the inclusive community we seek must be embodied in the community we practise

Together with our staff, we are responsible for:
- Our islands residential centres of Iona Abbey, the MacLeod Centre on Iona, and Camas Adventure Centre on the Ross of Mull

and in Glasgow:
- The administration of the Community
- Our work with young people
- Our publishing house, Wild Goose Publications
- Our association in the revitalising of worship with the Wild Goose Resource Group

The Iona Community was founded in Glasgow in 1938 by George MacLeod, minister, visionary and prophetic witness for peace, in the context of the poverty and despair of the Depression. Its original task of rebuilding the monastic ruins of Iona Abbey became a sign of hopeful rebuilding of community in Scotland and beyond. Today, we are about 250 Members, mostly in Britain, and 1500 Associate Members, with 1400 Friends worldwide. Together and apart, 'we follow the light we have, and pray for more light'.

For information on the Iona Community contact:
The Iona Community, Fourth Floor, Savoy House, 140 Sauchiehall Street,
Glasgow G2 3DH, UK. Phone: 0141 332 6343
e-mail: ionacomm@gla.iona.org.uk; web: www.iona.org.uk

For enquiries about visiting Iona, please contact:
Iona Abbey, Isle of Iona, Argyll PA76 6SN, UK. Phone: 01681 700404
e-mail: ionacomm@iona.org.uk

Printed in the United Kingdom
by Lightning Source UK Ltd.
110518UKS00001B/181-228